A. MACMECHAN B. A., PH. D.

IN THE GREAT DAYS OF SAIL

 14 SEA STORIES

ARCHIBALD MACMECHAN

EDITED BY ELIZABETH PEIRCE

NIMBUS
PUBLISHING

Nimbus Publishing Limited
3731 Mackintosh St, Halifax, NS B3K 5A5
(902) 455-4286 nimbus.ca

Printed and bound in Canada
Cover and interior design: John van der Woude
Cover image: "H.M.S. *Shannon* Leading Her Prize Into Halifax Harbour,
ca. 1830," by John Christian Schetky (1778–1874), W. H. Coverdale
collection of Canadiana, Manoir Richilieu collection, Library and
Archives Canada, copy negative C-041824.

Library and Archives Canada Cataloguing in Publication
MacMechan, Archibald, 1862-1933
In the great days of sail : 14 sea stories /
Archibald MacMechan ; edited by Elizabeth Peirce.
ISBN 978-1-55109-821-0
1. Sea stories, Canadian (English). 2. Seafaring life—Nova Scotia.
I. Peirce, Elizabeth, 1975- II. Title.
FC2311.M36 2011   971.6   C2010-908144-7

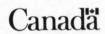 

Nimbus Publishing acknowledges the financial support for its publishing activities from the Government of Canada through the Canada Book
Fund (CBF) and the Canada Council for the Arts, and from the Province
of Nova Scotia through the Department of Communities, Culture and
Heritage.

ACKNOWLEDGEMENTS

My thanks to Linda MacLeod of the Dalhousie University Archives, home of the MacMechan collection; and Janet Baker, MacMechan biographer and faithful friend.

NOTES ON THE STORIES

The stories in this collection first appeared in book form in four collections by Archibald MacMechan which are now out of print. "The Captain's Boat," "Jordan the Pirate," and "Via London" were published in *Sagas of the Sea* (Toronto: Dent, 1923); "At the Harbour Mouth," "The Glory of the *Shannon*," "The *Saladin* Pirates," "The Saga of 'Rudder' Churchill," and "The *Sarah* Stands By" in *Old Province Tales* (Toronto: McClelland and Stewart, 1924); "The First Mate," "The Captain's Wife," "A Vision of the Night," "The Shell," "The Lunenburg Way," and "The Wave" in *There Go the Ships* (Toronto: McClelland and Stewart, 1928); and "The Ballad of the *Rover*" in the poetry collection *Late Harvest* (Toronto: Ryerson Press, 1934).

CONTENTS

Archibald MacMechan (left) and Boyd Dunham with a model of the
W. D. Lawrence

A FAITHFUL CHRONICLER:
THE LIFE AND WORK OF
ARCHIBALD MACMECHAN

Once counted among Nova Scotia's best-known writers, Archibald McKellar MacMechan was also a professor, literary critic, and archivist. His literary career was long and fruitful.

He began life on June 21, 1862, in Berlin (now Kitchener), Ontario, the eldest son of John MacMechan, a Presbyterian minister, and his wife, Mary Jean (McKellar) MacMechan. Upon the death of his mother in childbirth in 1870, young "Archie," as he was affectionately known, was sent to live with his grandfather McKellar in Hamilton. In 1880, he entered the University of Toronto as a modern languages student and after his graduation in 1884, taught school for two years in Brockville and Galt, Ontario, before entering Johns Hopkins University in 1886 as a doctoral candidate in modern languages. In 1889, the newly minted Dr. MacMechan married Edith May Cowan of Gananoque. In the same year, he accepted a professorship in the English department at Dalhousie University and moved to Halifax, the city where he would spend the rest of his life.

As an academic, MacMechan was a respected and often-published figure in Canadian letters. His 1896 edition of Thomas Carlyle's *Sartor Resartus* was for many years the standard. He edited a collection of Tennyson's poetry in 1907 and was an early and enthusiastic reviewer of Melville's then-overlooked classic

Moby Dick. A self-styled "Victorian sentimentalist," MacMechan was also an appreciative reader of Virginia Woolf's feminist classic "A Room of One's Own." His correspondence with Melville and Woolf is held at the Dalhousie University Archives at the Killam Memorial Library, several floors above the auditorium that bears his name, a tribute to his years as the university's librarian. Among his distinguished students were Lucy Maud Montgomery, Ernest Buckler, Hugh MacLennan, and Helen Creighton, all significant contributors in their own right to the literature and culture of the Maritime provinces. Though an unabashed imperialist and admirer of all things British, MacMechan was also a proud Canadian and clearly recognized the importance of a national literature. In 1924, McClelland and Stewart published MacMechan's well-regarded anthology *Headwaters of Canadian Literature*; the high standards the anthologist held for the literature under consideration is obvious from his words: "Only those rare works which combine deep knowledge of life, dramatic power to represent it and style, have a chance to survive." (*Headwaters*, 141 qtd in Baker 113). MacMechan's important contributions to Canadian letters were recognized by an honorary degree from the University of Toronto in 1920; in 1931, the year of his retirement from Dalhousie, he also received the Lorne Pierce medal from the Royal Society of Canada in recognition of distinguished service to Canadian literature.

It was his academic career that first brought MacMechan to Nova Scotia as a young man, but a solely academic life could not keep the indefatigable Archie occupied for long. As he approached middle age, MacMechan's interests shifted as his passion for Canadian history seemed to take precedence over more scholarly pursuits. His weekly review column in the *Montreal Standard*, begun in 1906 and running for the next twenty-seven years, had brought MacMechan's writing to a large, popular audience. His knowledge of Nova Scotia's rich history and his appreciation for the value of primary source material were evident in the works he wrote and edited, from the eighteenth century government records of Annapolis Royal to *The Winning of Popular Government*. In 1917, after the Halifax Explosion had laid waste much of MacMechan's beloved city, he served as director of the Halifax Disaster Record Office whose unenviable task it was to prepare an official account of the disaster. As part of his job, MacMechan spent many weeks interviewing survivors and documenting their painful experiences; these firsthand accounts of the frightening human toll of the Explosion, now housed at the Nova Scotia Public Archives and Records Management in Halifax, are an invaluable resource to the researcher.

It was as a chronicler of Nova Scotia's seafaring past that MacMechan was perhaps best known in his lifetime. Like another transplanted Nova Scotian, the celebrated folksinger Stan Rogers, MacMechan was devoted to his adopted province, a devotion which infused much of his writing. From our twenty-first century vantage point, it is difficult to imagine what the city of Halifax would have looked like to Archibald MacMechan during the closing years of the Victorian era and the tumultuous opening decades of the twentieth century, a period in which he was a firsthand witness to the steady decline of the golden age of sail. Small wonder that many of MacMechan's writings about Nova Scotia seem tinged with nostalgia for a vanishing way of life in the province, its ghostly presence still clearly visible to the chronicler's keen eye in the streets and buildings of the old port city. As his admirer Thomas Raddall remarked, "His knowledge of the old seaport and its long romantic story was so complete that for him, when he chose, the present time did not exist; he could ignore the clerks and shopgirls…who scurried past intent upon the petty worries of the twentieth century and see only the redcoats, the buckskin-clad rangers and tarry seamen of the eighteenth…. [He walked] the streets of Halifax in a curious, aloof way as if he had them all to himself" (Foreword, *Tales of the Sea*, vii).

This "kindly, courtly" figure observed by the young Raddall saw the great loss to the province represented by the passing away of the last eyewitnesses to Nova Scotia's shipping past, when towering ships like the *W. D. Lawrence*—Canada's largest sailing vessel when it was launched in 1874—were built in small villages like South Maitland and sailed around the world, making their owners fortunes, or breaking them. MacMechan recognized that stories of those times still lived among old sailors and their families in many Nova Scotian communities and he set himself the task of recording them. In the years following World War One, MacMechan travelled to many of these communities himself, interviewing shipbuilders, captains, crew members, and their descendants, gathering papers, maps, models, sketches, and photographs to add to his store of "tales," gripping, true-life accounts of danger, privation, and survival at sea in spite of unbelievable odds. The voluminous notes and multi-year correspondence with the subjects of these chronicles, now held at the Dalhousie University Archives, attest to MacMechan's meticulousness as a researcher intent on getting his facts straight. Three collections of stories gleaned by MacMechan were published in the 1920s: *Old Province Tales, Sagas of the Sea*, and *There Go The Ships*, all popular successes at the time of their release, though they are now out of print.

As another editor of MacMechan's sea stories, John Bell, aptly puts it, "If he did nothing else, we would be indebted to MacMechan for having the foresight to salvage so much of importance relating to such a significant period of our history. Our debt is much greater, however, because he was a master storyteller" (Bell, *At The Harbour Mouth,* 10). In his retelling of these stories, it is easy to detect MacMechan's admiration for the indomitable spirit of the Bluenose sailor, as well as his patriotism and idealistic fervour. Himself a product of the nineteenth century, MacMechan clearly identifies with the hardy individuals he writes about, while allowing their heroic deeds to speak for themselves. The stories reprinted here are MacMechan at his best and most compelling.

In his own words, from the opening of one of the stories in this collection: "The memory of brave deeds well done should not be allowed to perish from the world for lack of a faithful chronicler."

There was never a more faithful chronicler than Archibald MacMechan.

Elizabeth Peirce
February 2010

"The Captain's Boat." Sketch by Donald Mackay, from Tales of the Sea.

THE CAPTAIN'S BOAT

I

PERSONS OF THE DRAMA

The deep-sea captains of Nova Scotia took their wives with them on their long voyages, and these stout-hearted women shared with their husbands the perils of great waters. The ship was their floating home: the big comfortable cabin, the nursery. Nova Scotian children had memories of sliding down the tilted cabin floor in a storm, of "northers" in Valparaiso, of watching a vast expanse of sail against the sky as they lay on the cabin top in halcyon weather.

No stauncher vessels ever floated than those built in Nova Scotian shipyards of Bay of Fundy spruce. Their keels furrowed every sea. The master mariners of the province were a race apart, intrepid, skilled, resourceful, strong in character, strict in discipline, kings of the quarterdeck. They met every chance of the treacherous sea with unshaken hearts. They might be dismasted in the Indian Ocean, or crushed in Arctic ice floes. Yellow fever might carry off their crews in Rio, or their cargo might catch fire off the Horn. One and all they proved equal to every emergency. Wrecks and disasters only threw into relief the heroism of captain and crew. They lived to tell the tale. But the common form of epitaph for many an able ship was "Never again heard of."

When the full-rigged ship *Milton* of fourteen hundred ton register was launched from the yard of Brown and Anthony of Maitland, Nova Scotia, in 1879, the captain's wife, Kate MacArthur, was on aboard, and for two years and a half she lived in the vessel that was her home, except for one week which she spent ashore at Copenhagen. She was no ordinary woman. Strong in body and mind, fair of face, educated, musical, observant, keen-witted, "the best of company," she was a devoted wife and mother. She took her religion to sea. The salt was in her blood. Her first voyage was to New Orleans, where their ship was burnt at the wharf edge.

The man of her choice was Henry MacArthur, like her born and brought up in Maitland. He was rather under middle size, powerfully built, with a cast in the right eye. His friends recognized his strength of character, and his life proved the truth of their estimate. Once in the North Atlantic his vessel became waterlogged, and he had to take to the rigging. He suffered many things before he was rescued, but he was saved to endure greater hardships in another ocean.

On August 9, 1881, the *Milton* sailed from Shields with a cargo of coal for San Francisco. There were twenty-three souls on board. Captain MacArthur had his wife with him and his two little boys, Archie, a fair-haired child of four, and Frankie, a mere baby of two. Charles Carroll of Windsor, N.S., was the first mate, and Edwin S. Anthony of Maitland, second. He was eighteen years of age and had spent five at sea. There were seventeen hands before the mast, for the *Milton* was one of the biggest and finest ships ever built in Nova Scotia. The voyage through the Atlantic, around the Horn, and into the Pacific was as pleasant as any in Kate MacArthur's experience. With good weather and favourable winds it stretched out into months, an endless succession of peaceful days. Day by day the magnificent big ship ploughed her stately way across the vast, empty sea. She was a new, staunch and well-found vessel, with a consummate sailor in command, and she had completed three-fourths of her course; but fate had prepared a tragic ending for the pleasant voyage.

The seaman's is the most perilous of callings. Death is always in ambush, waiting to spring upon him.

II
TAKING TO THE BOATS

All went well until December 22. The *Milton* was just north of the Equator: to be precise, in latitude 3° north, longitude 110° west. Dinner was over in the cabin, when Carroll, the first mate, hurried in with the dread news that the cargo of coal was on fire. Someone had noticed smoke coming up the main hatch. Even in a dump exposed to the air, coal generates heat and gas. Packed in a ship's hold it is a dangerous cargo. The first warning of danger may be flames bursting through a bulkhead, or an explosion which tears the hatches off the deck. There is no greater terror than fire at sea.

3

At the time Captain MacArthur was in bed, crippled with rheumatism, "hardly able to move a finger." His wife had to help him to dress, but he was soon on deck. He got the force pumps working and organized a bucket brigade. All that afternoon and far into the night the crew of the *Milton* fought the fire, but in vain. The hold was a burning furnace under their feet. They did all that men could do, but they could not save the stately *Milton;* and at four bells MacArthur gave the order to hoist out the boats. At three o'clock in the morning of December 23 they were forced to leave her. "We all got away ship-shape and Bristol fashion."

The three boats were lowered and supplied with everything needed for a long voyage—bedding, water, tinned provisions. The weather was calm; there was time to get all necessary stores together. MacArthur was "practical," as a fellow-captain put it. He thought of everything. He took with him the ship's register, that indispensable document without which a captain never goes ashore, his chart of the North Pacific (which Mrs. MacArthur carried in her bosom), his sextant, the ship's compass and the patent log. He kept a record of the long voyage about to begin, a document still in his son Archie's possession. He even took with him his red ensign, and it served a practical purpose in the end.

The captain's boat was twenty-four feet long, seven and a half feet in beam, and three and a half feet deep—the dimensions of a small yacht. She was fitted with two masts carrying sprit-sails and a jib. Into this roomy boat went all necessary gear and provisions of canned goods and hard biscuit for twenty-five days, including the chest of linen bought in Belfast by the captain's wife. Mrs. MacArthur and the two little boys followed. She had no fear, or even nervousness at the prospect of the perilous adventure on which she was embarking, though she was soon to bear another child. The carpenter, Johansen, two foremast hands, Anderson and Annesitt, and the boatswain, George Ettinger, a Nova Scotian boy from Kennetcook, went with them.

Into the first mate's boat went seven men, including the cook. She was fitted with two sprit-sails but no jib. The boat of Edwin Anthony, the second mate, was called the captain's gig. It was long and narrow and carried a single sprit-sail. It was used for going ashore and when at anchor in the stream or in harbour. It did not require the same sail as the others to get up the same speed. All three boats were provisioned alike.

They rowed off about a mile to windward of the ship, as MacArthur feared an explosion of gas, and for the rest of the tropic night they watched the *Milton* flaming like a huge torch, and lighting up leagues of ocean. At daylight the flames burst through the deck. They rowed back to the ship, and MacArthur the practical tried to increase his stock of provisions. Carroll, the first mate, was ordered on board for this end, but he could not get at the stores for the smoke and heat.

The three boats did not begin their voyage at once. Throughout the whole of December 23, and until the next morning, they stood by and watched the flaming ship. By that time the masts and upper deck were gone. The *Milton* was burnt to the water's edge. The woman gives one reason for this strange reluctance to part from the ship they could not save:

"She seemed company to us out there on the Pacific. She was a fine ship and we loved her as our home. It seemed such a pity to see her go to ruin right there before our eyes."

It was like a true sailor's wife to forget her own desperate plight in regret for the ruined ship. Another reason for waiting was the chance of the fire attracting the attention of a passing vessel. The *Milton* was only a dismantled, smoking, glowing hulk when the three boats started in procession northward for the nearest land, Cape St. Lucas, at the very tip of Lower California. The captain's boat was in the lead and at night burned the ship's port or red light, showing astern. The second mate's followed the captain's and showed the starboard or green light over the stem. The first mate's boat came third in the forlorn little flotilla, and the boat ahead had no means of knowing that the next astern was following and keeping station.

The starting point for their long voyage was not favourable. Their destination was twelve hundred miles due north. Their course lay across the Equatorial Current, which would carry them eastward, and the Counter Equatorial Current, which would carry them westward. After that, there was a long disheartening beating up against the northeast trades to follow. The navigation of the smallest vessel with the simplest rig means continual vigilance. Conditions of sea and wind and weather vary from hour to hour. MacArthur had first to determine what course he should sail in order to take advantage of the favourable winds and lose the minimum of time and distance. This was a problem for the experienced navigator. MacArthur solved it triumphantly.

The presence of his wife and children must have increased his anxieties tenfold. Before the end, he had to suffer the extremes of hunger and thirst, to witness those nearest and dearest endure the same torments, to watch his baby boy die. Before the end, his long vigils and the dazzling brightness of the sun on the tropic seas affected his eyesight and produced a most painful malady. He found the foreigners were not to be trusted. Before the end, he had to keep up the morale of despairing, mutinous, insane men. Still he held on, never bating a jot of heart or hope, even when hope seemed folly. And his iron will won through.

The boats soon parted company. On Christmas Eve, the first mate's boat luffed up alongside Anthony's and Carroll "passed the usual good night and Merry Christmas and dropped astern again. I supposed he was following, but when daylight broke on Christmas morning nothing could be seen of his boat. We cruised about all day, but did not sight the mate's boat again, and since that time she has not been heard of. He was a fine fellow and a good seaman, but in a careless moment must have held her in the trough and filled her or turned her over, as the breeze was fresh and one had to be looking for combers all the time and let her head come to the wind to avoid filling."

The two remaining boats resumed their voyage. The weather was fine. An awning was rigged over the after part of the long-boat, so that Mrs. MacArthur could have some shelter and privacy. Here she slept with her children. Often she would ask the captain to leave the awning aside so that she could lie and watch the tropic stars. At such times she wondered if she should ever see the folk in quiet little Maitland again.

There was no suffering from cold, though all were frequently wet to the skin with the water shipped in rough weather. The heat of the morning sun would draw up a thick white steam from the bedding, and it soon rotted.

On the ninth day there was another parting of company. In Anthony's own words, "I awoke to find I had lost sight of the captain's boat, and by inquiry from the A.B. who steered the last trick, found that he had not passed the captain's boat, but had allowed it to get out of sight dead ahead. So there was nothing to do but crowd on sail and overhaul it if we could, which we did in a few hours, as the captain had missed us and lay-to for us to come up. Well, when I came alongside he hailed me and asked me to come on his boat as he wanted to have a talk with me. I reluctantly went over and the steward stepped in my place. He was a Dane, an experienced seaman and navigator and one who had seen better days; probably he walked the weather side, but was in the lee scuppers when we shipped him. When it came night the captain said, 'You can go on your boat in the morning, but stay with me tonight; my wife and the boys want to talk with you.' So I did, and when day broke there was no second boat in sight." As in the former case, the longboat cruised about all day looking for her missing consort and only gave up the search when darkness settled on the water.

On the twenty-third day, the crew of the second mate's boat were picked up by the British ship *Cochin* and taken to San Francisco, bringing the first news of the disaster.

This transfer, which was apparently the result of chance, worked well. MacArthur had a man of his own race to relieve him at the tiller, one who understood navigation, and who could take his place in case of accident. Foreigners are always doubtful, and in the event of trouble they would be two to one. His captain's confidence in the Maitland boy was well justified. Edwin Anthony knew how to obey, and in more than one emergency rendered valuable assistance.

On the morning of January 4, 1882, MacArthur made a startling discovery. "I found the provisions and water were becoming scarce, and from this day put all hands on short allowance." Behind this unemotional statement is the ugly fact that the hands were pilfering the food and drinking the water in the night. Foreseeing the dangers of thirst, MacArthur took no salt provisions except one ham for each boat. Everything else was in tins. The sailors would purloin a can of tomatoes, for instance, from the stores, pierce it with a nail, drink off the liquid, and replace it. When the time came to open the tin, the contents had rotted. It was a sickening discovery of suicidal treachery. Henceforth the mate and captain had to keep watch and ward over their scanty stock of food and water by day and night.

One seems to see a sunburnt, bearded figure with bloodshot eyes steering his big boat northward, ever northward, with his revolver ready to his hand. Under the rude awning are his wife and children, and forward the cowed and treacherous foreigners.

The Pacific is a vast and empty ocean, traversed at that time by few ships. Not until the morning of January 16 did the castaways of the *Milton* sight a sail. Their position was latitude 19° 58' north and longitude 121° 55' west. The strange vessel was six miles to the north of them, standing to the eastward. The captain's boat was on the opposite tack. MacArthur came about in order to cross the stranger's track, but there was a rough sea and little wind. To help the boat along he put the men at the oars, and to strengthen and encourage them at their hard task he gave them two gallons of water out of their scanty store. The captain had no doubt at the time that they were seen and would be picked up, so he could afford to be lavish. He watched the strange sail try to come about, miss stays, and then "wear," or come round in the opposite direction, as if she had seen the boat with the British ensign flying union down and was heading directly for it. Hope of rescue was strong in every heart.

Then at the critical moment a squall swept down across the face of the water, blurring sky and sea. The stranger wore round with his head to the northwest, and quickly disappeared from sight.

The castaways stood up and waved signals, and shouted till their voices failed. All was in vain. The hope of rescue vanished beyond the sea-rim.

For the honour of the unknown master of the unknown vessel, MacArthur, with the chivalry of the sea, records his conviction that the stranger did not see the *Milton*'s boat; otherwise he would have picked them up.

III

THE CONDENSER

It was a cruel disappointment. Weakened by the short allowance of food, worn out with pulling at the oars, the men "lost heart," as their captain records, "and gave up." But MacArthur was the breed that never gives up or gives in, the kind that fights on with the scabbard when the sword is broken.

On January 18 the last drop of water was gone. The single precious gallon remaining had been husbanded and doled out justly, cupful by cupful, share and share alike. Then the more dreadful tortures of thirst began.

Hunger is easier to bear than thirst. After the first three or four days of slow starvation, the feeling of hunger passes away. The body falls back on its reserves, and consumes first its fat and then its muscle. It wastes to skin and bone. Weakness comes on, and listlessness increases as strength fails. But thirst is an agony always intensifying and culminating in madness.

9

Kate MacArthur tells a little of what she endured: "My tongue got thick and stuck out between my cracked lips, and I seemed burning for water. I used to get a little relief by binding my head and throat with cloths dipped in the sea, but still the thirst kept raging worse and worse."

The fable of King Tantalus up to the lips in water he might not drink was a reality in the captain's boat. To drink of the sun-lit, sparkling brine was madness. Rain fell all around the horizon from time to time, but no shower blessed the baked lips of the castaways. Memories of far-off Maitland thronged on the captain's wife to increase her misery.

"As I lay in the bottom of the boat with the little sufferers and heard the swish of the sea against the side, the memory of every drink I had ever enjoyed came back to tantalize me. I don't believe I ever took a drink of cool water, from my childhood up to the moment of leaving the ship, that each circumstance did not come back to my mind distinctly. And to look at all that water around us, so blue and clear and cool when we dipped our hands in the sea, it seemed very strange that we should be dying of thirst."

Sleep brought no relief. One dream haunted her—of standing by a well of cold water and putting the cup to her lips. The sailors were insanely drinking seawater at night; the children were moaning for water. And there was no water.

MacArthur and Anthony between them made a condenser, "after a great deal of trouble." This exploit is, one would say, unique in the annals of shipwreck.

It consisted of three parts: a tomato can with a cover in which the water was boiled, a tube fitted into it and running through a second can of cold water to condense the steam. This rude still was secured to the after-thwart by lashings of marlin. The two problems were the "worm," and fuel for the fire. After forty years Mr. Anthony writes: "That tube I remember well. It was made from a tin can, cut in a long strip, as when you pare an apple round and round without breaking the peel, and spirally constructed, as you would wrap a strip of paper about an inch wide around a pencil, with a half-inch lap, so that half the width of the strip was in the lap. The diameter of the tube was about one-quarter or three-eighths of an inch. This tube was fitted to the condenser can and to the cooling can, being wound with cloth and marlin. The joint connecting the tube with the condenser was made tight."

But how could the indispensable fire be built and maintained? For fireplace the cover of Mrs. MacArthur's old-fashioned tin or sheet-metal trunk was torn off and secured under the can for boiling water. For fuel MacArthur literally burnt his boat under him. He whittled up all the oars but two. Then he attacked the planking, the "ribbons," the thwarts, the gunwales. Every particle of wood that could be spared without weakening the structure of the boat was used to feed the fire. Only the central thwart was spared. In this way he managed to obtain from a pint to almost a quart of water in twenty-four hours. Henceforth there is always fine, acrid, hardwood smoke drifting to leeward, as the longboat is held down on her predestined course. The fire is maintained like the fire of Vesta.

"We used to sit and count the drops, as the condensed water dripped into the tin," said the captain's wife; and the second mate confirms.

A mouthful of water in the twenty-four hours barely held life in the body. All shared alike. The condenser was kept going, the boat was navigated, observations were taken, position fixed, and progress recorded in the log by the will of the gaunt, bearded man with bloodshot eyes. The lives of all depended on him. That is the captain's part.

One night there was trouble with one of the hands. Anthony recalls the incident: "I remember distinctly, one night when I was at the tiller, seeing a Greek worming his way aft on his stomach, evidently bent on securing food or causing trouble. I touched Captain MacArthur with my foot, he being asleep at the time, and he understood immediately. A club we had near for such an emergency was used immediately, and this Greek was stowed away unconscious in the bow of the boat. We also discovered that he had a very vicious-looking knife. Strange to say, this man was the only one of the sailors to survive."

Then death entered the longboat. The youngest was first to go. Said the captain's wife:

"My little boys began to cry for water. My two-year-old baby Frankie lay moaning out of his parched mouth and died in my lap of hunger and thirst. It was too much...too much."

But the mother could not weep for him then. To a friend MacArthur said afterwards, "I would have given my life to give him water." Anthony's narrative states the blood was running from the baby's mouth.

Frankie died on February 2, but the mother could not bear to have the wasted little body put over the side and dropped into the sea. Sharks were always dogging the boat. MacArthur sewed up his child's body in canvas and placed it in a tin box to be taken ashore and given Christian burial.

The food so carefully husbanded and so insanely pilfered came to an end at last. There remained the ham as emergency ration. It was portioned out justly, share and share alike. Everyone in the boat fared the same, captain, child, and common sailor. Only shreds of meat were left on the ham bone.

On January 28 a big flying fish rose out of the sea and fell into the boat. It was cooked and eaten, affording each a mouthful. That was the last of the food.

All through this dread voyage the mother denied herself for her children's sake. That is the mother's part. Kate MacArthur merely nibbled at her portion and gave what she could to her wailing babes. For two weeks at the end she hoarded a morsel of hard biscuit for the surviving child, against an emergency.

On February 5, Ole Johansen, the carpenter, died, just before the rescue came.

IV
THE RESCUE

Early in the morning of February 6, MacArthur made his landfall. He sighted St. Roque Island, a small barren rock nearly five hundred miles north of Cape St. Lucas. He had used the northeast trades to work as far west as longitude 120° 50', and as far north as latitude 28° 50', far out of his course, to the landsman's eye. Then reaching the region of variable winds, he was able to make a much more advantageous slant for the coast of California. The longboat had been held inexorably upon her predetermined course of 2,619 miles for forty-six days by the master mind. Despite the perils of wind and sea, despite sickness, hunger, thirst, weakness, disappointment, mutiny, death itself, the captain had reached the land he sought, and he had made assurance doubly sure. His admiring second mate calls him "a wonderful navigator," and this feat justifies his praise.

Though land was in sight, the castaways had still to suffer much from hope deferred. The coast was bold and rocky. MacArthur headed the boat south in search of a harbour. No landing could be effected. No one in the boat was of any real use but the two Nova Scotians. The man who had risen from a sick bed to fight fire, who had endured the extremity of hunger, thirst, and pain, who bore the whole weight of responsibility, was, at the end of the ordeal, the strongest man in the boat. Loyal Edwin Anthony was so weak as to be hardly fit for duty. The three sailors, mere skin and bone, were lying helpless in the bottom of the boat.

Evening fell. Then in the gathering dusk, about half past seven, MacArthur sighted a schooner about five miles to the eastward. He made every endeavour to reach the stranger, but the wind failed, and he could not come up with her. The night closed down and the sail of hope was lost to view. For the second time rescue seemed close at hand, and for the second time, it vanished like a dream. "We were in despair."

This was the time that even Kate MacArthur's brave heart failed her. She begged her husband to pull the plug out of the bottom of the boat and put a period to their long-drawn agony. Drowning is a speedy and not a very hard death. MacArthur answered, "We will wait a little longer."

Two long hours passed. MacArthur lowered his sails and waited, pitching and tossing on the rough sea. His bloodshot eyes were straining through the darkness for a glimpse of the vanished sail. And then he made out vaguely the dim shape of the schooner in the gloom. In the two hours of waiting she had drawn much nearer to the boat. The wind dropped. Both craft were becalmed. MacArthur set his living skeletons rowing the longboat towards the schooner. He records, "It was with great difficulty that I could come up to her."

For a whole hour they toiled, shouting at the same time to attract the attention of the schooner's crew. Rescue was close at hand. The last remnants of their strength went into their frantic efforts to reach the ark of safety.

No answering hail came from the schooner until the boat was within one length of her, but the exhausted men had not the strength to pull those last few yards. Then someone shouted in Spanish and MacArthur replied, "I have lost my ship and have been cast away for forty-six days in the boat. We are perishing for water and food."

The schooner captain flung him a line by which the boat was hauled alongside. Then, suddenly, he slacked off the line, dropping the boat some forty feet astern. The breeze freshened, the schooner's sails filled, and the boat began to tow in her wake. Next, without a word of warning, the line was cut, and a gun was fired from the schooner which forged ahead while the boat drifted rapidly astern.

What possible reason could there be for such inhuman treatment? To all in the boat, these seemed the acts of cruel madmen. In the darkness, hope of rescue died down again. A whole hour passed. It was now near midnight.

Then occurred another strange incident in this nightmare experience. Two men in a skiff rowed alongside. They had come from the schooner with a breaker of water which they passed into the longboat. The jabbering foreigners could give no explanation, but their intentions were evidently friendly. Mrs. MacArthur and her little boy got into the skiff; and then, to her consternation, the men rowed away with them into the darkness. The mystery of the strangers' actions were deepening every minute. How could their conduct be explained?

Soon the skiff reached the schooner's side, and the two passengers were taken on board. Mrs. MacArthur's condition must have been plain to every eye. The captain gave her a little wine to restore her. Speaking Spanish, for the stranger captain did not speak English, she made him understand, more by tears perhaps than words, that she wanted to be taken back to her husband in the derelict boat, lying off somewhere in the night.

The Spanish captain hesitated. He talked with his men, and Mrs. MacArthur standing by caught the drift of what they were saying. They knew that pirates were lurking about Cerros Island, whither they were bound; and when the big boat appeared mysteriously from nowhere, hailing them frantically in the darkness, they thought they had to deal with a gang of cutthroats attempting to seize their vessel. They drew their knives and prepared for a desperate resistance.

Mrs. MacArthur's Spanish was sufficient to make the captain understand the true situation. The mysterious boat was not manned by pirates but by shipwrecked sailors at the point of death. As soon as he understood, he sent the skiff off again. That last hour must have been the most anxious that MacArthur knew in all the voyage, but in the end he had the relief of seeing the skiff return. It made fast to the big boat and towed it back to the schooner, where all the castaways were taken on board. The vessel which had rescued them proved to be the *Thor*, Captain Christobal Sosa, with a Mexican crew, bound up the coast for a cargo of dye-stuffs. MacArthur states: "As soon as they became satisfied that I intended them no harm, they treated me and my poor starving crew with the greatest kindness and consideration, and during my stay on board their kindness never ceased."

But the rescue was signalized by one more death. Worn out by his long vigils, privations, sufferings, MacArthur sat down on the deck of the *Thor* and leaned against the side of the cabin.

For the first time since the alarm of fire on board the *Milton,* the burden of responsibility slipped from him, and he fell asleep. He had warned his men against drinking freely of the water in their exhausted condition. The two Nova Scotians heeded the warning, but Tilly Anderson, able seaman, mad with thirst, crawled to the water cask, worried the bung out, drank his fill, and, in spite of all that could be done for him, died the next day.

For three days, from February 6–9, the survivors of the *Milton* remained on board the *Thor.* The kindness of the Mexicans was great; they made ample amends for their previous mistakes, but the poor fellows had little to share with their guests. There was nothing to eat but "awful black bread." On February 9 they were a few miles south of Cerros Island, when they sighted the smoke of a steamer. For the first time in her regular trips, this vessel was passing on this particular side of the island. As she neared the *Thor,* MacArthur ran up his ensign union down, and the steamer immediately changed her course and made for the signal of distress.

When she came within a mile, MacArthur placed his sick men in the longboat, and the crew of the *Thor* rowed them off to the waiting steamer. She proved to be the American passenger steamer *Newbern,* in command of Captain Thomas Huntington, from San Francisco, bound up the Gulf of California. They were taken on board and received every kindness. The two sailors, Annesitt and Ettinger, could not rise from the bottom of the boat and had to be lifted on board. Ettinger died a few hours afterwards. Captain MacArthur and Archie were in better condition than any of the others. Edwin Anthony and Mrs. MacArthur required no assistance in getting up the side. As she went up the companionway, she heard a passenger exclaim:

"Oh! look at that poor squaw, so black and weatherbeaten."

It was four weeks before she could get the tangles out of her hair, but when she was interviewed in San Francisco, sixteen days later, she was recovering her looks. To the reporter she appeared "a pleasant, mild-spoken woman, with light hair, grey eyes, and cheeks on which the roses were struggling out through the tan of her exposure, and the pallor of her terrible suffering and sickness, although she was very weak and reduced in flesh."

The tragic longboat of the *Milton*, whittled and scarred but still staunch, was given to the *Thor*, but the ship's compass was presented to the *Newbern*.

Two incidents come into the sequel. As the *Newbern* was entering Guyamas harbour on February 16, Mrs. MacArthur's baby was born. He was named Newbern Huntington after the steamer and the captain. Though weighing only three pounds at birth, the boy grew to manhood and is now a distinguished physician in California. On the evening of Saturday, February 25, Mrs. MacArthur was being interviewed in the Devon House, Market Street, San Francisco. She had Newbern in her lap, with Archie, "a rosy-cheeked, blue-eyed, chubby boy in a sailor suit," playing about the room and occasionally joining in the conversation. She told the *Chronicle* reporter:

"I can't say that I ever completely gave up hope. I knew that we were under good protection and in safe hands, for I counted that God saw us and cared for us."

Captain MacArthur's eye trouble was caused in part by the strain of taking sights with the sextant in a pitching, tossing boat. During the last week of the voyage, Anthony relieved him by making the daily observation. There was inflammation and great pain. He went to a San Francisco oculist for the necessary operation. Refusing to take chloroform, he gripped the arms of the chair he sat in and endured the pain without wincing, while streams of blood and pus ran down his cheeks. When it was all over, MacArthur asked about the fee. The answer was, "Nothing, to a man like you."

La Tribune *and* Unicorn *in battle, 1796. Painting by an unknown artist.*

AT THE HARBOUR MOUTH

The entrance to Halifax Harbour is blocked by a large irregular island, which leaves to the westward a mile wide passage between itself and the mainland. The shallow, twisting eastern passage is used only by small fishing craft, but this western passage is the water gate of the old city, through which the great ships come and go. The mainland is one granite cliff, steep and high. Its summit is crowned by an old-fashioned round fort with battlements, called York Redoubt, which has been an imperial signal station for more than a century. Modern engineers have made it a second Gibraltar, but that is by the way. At the heel of the island, to seaward, is a low windworn dune called Thrum Cap, from which series of shoals run out for half a mile. When the southeast winds blow hard, the great waves trip upon these ledges and wall the harbour mouth with breakers. The fishermen still call the outermost reef the Tribune Shoal, from events which took place there more than a century ago.

On November 23, 1797, about the hour of nine, two men standing outside the gates of York Redoubt and looking seaward saw a fine large frigate, under British colours, bowling along with a steady wind straight for the fair-lying entrance. One of the men was Lieutenant Brenton Halliburton of the 7th Fusiliers, the Duke of Kent's own regiment, afterwards Sir Brenton Halliburton, chief justice of Nova Scotia, and the other was Sergeant McCormack of the same famous corps. They watched the nearing ship closely, and the sergeant, who knew the shoals as well as any tar on board, saw that she was standing into danger.

"If that ship does not alter her course," he said, "she will be aground in a quarter of an hour."

He was too liberal in his time allowance. Within five minutes, the watchers on the cliff saw the good ship check and stop short, as the granite hand of the reef laid firm hold of her keel. The cloud of canvas, instead of filling gracefully, tore frantically this way and that, and the wind carried the noise of the thunderous flapping to the cliff. The tall masts canted over to leeward, and the waves she rode so proudly a moment before now leaped over the bulwarks and swept the decks. The frigate was hard aground on the Thrum Cap shoals.

It was an annoying accident, and it need not have happened. The ship in trouble had only lately come into the possession of His Britannic Majesty, George the Third. She had been built in some French dockyard by good republican shipwrights and launched with a brave revolutionary name, *La Tribune,* to do battle with perfidious Albion. On June 8, 1796, however, she had fallen a prey to HMS *Unicorn* after a chase of two hundred miles and now was manned with a British crew. In September of 1797, she had formed part of the guard to convoy the Quebec and Newfoundland fleet from Torbay across the Atlantic. By stress of weather, she had been separated from the merchantmen, and early that morning, far out at sea, the mastheads had descried the Nova Scotia coast.

About eight o'clock on this eventful morning, the commander, Captain Scory Barker, paced the quarterdeck. "Don't you think, Mr. Club," he said to his sailing master, "that it would be advisable to lie-to and signal for a pilot?"

Mr. Club did not agree with his superior officer. He knew the harbour; the wind was fair. Not long since he had worked a forty-four gun ship in, in the teeth of a gale; it would save time, and so on.

Captain Barker hesitated. He knew what was prudent and what ugly consequences followed on the British captains' errors of judgment. Admirals had been shot on the deck of their own ships and victorious officers courtmartialled for the very devices by which they gained their victories. England expected her sailors to be infallible. In the navy there is no forgiveness of sins.

At this moment, Mr. John Galvin, master's mate, a passenger, was taking the air on deck. He overheard the colloquy, and spoke up.

"If Captain Barker would accept of my services, I should be happy to assist Mr. Club in taking the ship in. I have had some experience of Halifax Harbour, sir."

This was an understatement. Mr. Galvin knew the harbour as well as you know your alphabet. But the one thing the British captain of that day could not brook was the faintest sign of interference.

"When your services are required, Mr. Galvin, it will be time enough to volunteer them. I consider Mr. Club quite competent to take the ship in."

Mr. Galvin's sallow, fever-shrivelled face went red. He had just been exchanged from a sickening French prison in Guadeloupe, where he had been chained leg and leg with his devoted friend, First Lieutenant Thomas Fennell. His health was not good; he drew himself up, bowed in silence, and went below to his cot.

Captain Barker also went below. He had papers to arrange before handing them over to the port admiral. There was much to be done before the *Tribune* should be snug at anchor off the dockyard. The sailing master, Mr. James Club, was left in charge of the deck, as well as several other things, such as Captain Barker's reputation and the lives of a whole ship's company. In spite of his assurances, Mr. Club was not perfectly certain of himself, but he knew that if luck favoured him he would get an allowance for pilotage in addition to his pay. So he put a leadsman in the bow-chains, and in the head he stationed a black sailor, John Casey, upon whose knowledge of the port he relied, to con the ship.

All went well for an hour. Then as the swift frigate washed on, the leadsman announced rapidly shoaling water. The black man's directions became uncertain.

"Desire Mr. Galvin to come on deck immediately," cried Club.

"We're standing into shoal water," he shouted to the black. "Which way now, Casey?"

"Mr. Club, for God, I don't know."

At this moment Galvin reached the deck. From the bows came the hoarse cry of the leadsman, "By the mark, five!"

The master, thoroughly alarmed, rushed to the wheel and took the spokes out of the steersman's hands, as if to wear ship. "How shall I put my helm, Mr. Galvin?" Galvin leaped on a carronade to get a sight of the ship's whereabouts, but his aid had been invoked too late. At that moment, the frigate struck and heeled over, and in place of the beautiful order of a ship under sail was unutterable confusion.

Captain Barker was on deck in an instant.

"A — nice job you've made of it, Mr. Club. You've lost the ship. And do you mean to say, sir," he added, catching sight of Galvin, "that you would stand by and see the master run the ship aground after all your officious palaver this morning?"

To such a just and seasonable question there was no possible reply, and Captain Barker was already shouting a dozen orders—to furl the sails—to sound the pumps—to make signals of distress. The crew swarmed on deck and up the yards. In a few minutes the canvas was all taken in, the carpenter reported very little water in the hold; the minute guns were booming, and from the ships in port seven miles away other guns answered.

It was an annoying accident; annoying, nothing more. The wind was rising, to be sure, and everything promised a storm. The situation of the ship was exposed and might become dangerous, but help was close at hand and would surely come from the dockyard, to which the wagging telegraph on York Redoubt soon told the news. The tide was coming in when the *Tribune* struck and if lightened she would float off at the top of the flood. Still Captain Barker was not happy. A few months before he had sat on a courtmartial which had dismissed a brother officer from the service for abandoning his ship, which had gone ashore, although he had saved the lives of his crew. England had a great war on her hands and could not spare a single ship. It was no comfort that the accident was not his fault and might have been avoided. He lost his head.

The tide was high that day at a quarter to twelve, and if the frigate was to get clear something must be done at once. Accordingly, one by one, the eighteen heavy guns on the starboard side were hoisted out at the yardarms, and one by one they splashed into the shoal water in her lee. Then down the slanting deck, the guns of the port broadside were lowered and dropped in the sea, except one, which was kept for signals; and all that afternoon the deep, heavy, melancholy sound of the signal gun firing at short intervals mingled with the noises of rising wind and dashing water. The manoeuvre was useless; the *Tribune* remained fast on the shoal, heeled over on her starboard side. Indeed, the manoeuvre was worse than useless; it was fatal, as the event proved; for, in the confusion, all the cannons were jettisoned in the lee of the ship, forming there a reef of tumbled iron on the granite, against which the *Tribune* was to break her bones.

The wind was rising to a gale from the southeast and the swelling seas battered the motionless ship with ever-increasing violence, breaking clean over her exposed quarter.

At last the long unexpected help arrived. One heavy barge, after a hard pull of seven miles, reached the stranded ship. Other boats had started but were forced to put back. But what was the rage and dismay of Captain Barker when he found that no one above the rank of a boatswain, one Rackum by name, had been sent to his aid. Admiral Murray had been recently superseded in the command of the station and he could, or would, issue no orders. There was no one to share with Captain Barker the responsibility of abandoning his ship. He flew into a rage with Rackum and would not speak peaceably to him. He even refused to allow the rescue party to quit the ship, much less one man of the crew. One of the army officers who had put off from one of the shore forts to render assistance pointed out that the gale was growing worse and worse, that it would not be high water until after dark, and that in the *Tribune*'s exposed position there was great danger of her going to pieces. He begged Captain Barker to land his crew, or at least the women and children.

"Ah, sir!" was the reply, "I wish your coat was blue instead of red. No! Not a soul quits this ship as long as two planks hold together."

So the edict went forth! Was he not a British captain, unquestioned despot on his own ship, where his word was law? There was no panic; discipline prevailed. The day wore on; nothing further could be done but wait, wait, wait the tedious tide. Seven miles away the good people of Halifax went about their business, ate their dinners, and took their ease; the admiral was attending a christening party, says tradition, while at the harbour mouth the tragedy of this doomed ship's company was played to its close.

At six o'clock the tide turned, and as it rose the *Tribune* began to roll to and fro on the shoal. The gloomy day ended in a stormy November night. Then another misfortune befell, for it seems as if relentless fate plucked away hope after hope from these ill-starred men, as a boy pulls an insect to pieces, a limb at a time. The vessel's stem was to the open sea and exposed through long hours to the fullest action of the waves. All afternoon moving hills of water leaped over the quarter and beat against the useless rudder. No bolts or chains could stand such a strain for ever. At last the fastenings parted and the waves wrenched the rudder from its place. With it went the last chance of saving the ship. Even then the crew might have been saved, but the needful order was not given. The rising tide and the waves together half lifted her and she lurched continually from side to side. The masts sloped over, the blocks rattled, the yards clamoured in their sailings, slings, and the wind screeched through the cordage. For upward of two hours, the unfortunate ship beat upon her own guns and stove in the planking on her starboard side.

About nine o'clock, driven by the gale, the *Tribune* slid off the shoal into deep water, afloat at last, but without a rudder and with seven feet of water in her hold. So she drifted in the dark before the southeast gale across two miles of raging water to Herring Cove.

Still every effort is made to save the ship. Her chain-pumps are clanking away as fast as sturdy arms can work them, but still the leak gains. Every moment the swaling hulk sinks lower and every moment brings her nearer the deadly lee shore. It is no time to stand on one's dignity. Captain Barker takes counsel with the despised boatswain as one who knows the harbour, and Rackum advises him to let go the bower anchor. It fails to grip the bottom and the battered frigate drifts nearer the granite cliffs, against which the waves are breaking twenty feet high. The doomed men try another desperate shift to save their lives. While the pumps clank on, some seamen cut the cable and others set the jib and fore topmast staysail. If they could but manage with her head canvas to nose inside the harbour mouth less than a mile away, they would be safe. But it is not easy to sail a waterlogged ship without a helm in a November storm. No expedient will bring up the drifting ship. When they are almost under the cliff, as a last desperate resource they drop the second anchor in thirteen fathoms of water. For a wonder it holds. To lighten her, the mizzen-mast is cut away; the *Tribune* rides a trifle easier, and there seems to be a faint hope that she may outlive the storm.

It is a vain hope; the *Tribune* is at her last moorings. After all her cruises, she has come to lay her bones at the foot of this wild Nova Scotian cliff. Now there is no escape for her. In sixty minutes after she floated at Thrum Cap, she crossed that two-mile stretch of water and brought up just three ship's lengths south of Herring Cove, a narrow, curving fissure in the iron coast. Today the banks are lined by a quaint fishing village, which then consisted of only a few scattered huts. The drifting *Tribune* just missed the entrance, and safety. About half past nine, she was observed to lurch violently twice and then go down all standing, as a ship does when she is evenly full of water. She carried down with her, not only her own crew, but some sailors' wives and children, and men sent from the dockyard to the ship's assistance. Some sank at once, and some were battered against the cliff. But the fore- and mainmasts remained well above water, and nearly one hundred survivors managed to get into the rigging.

It was only a temporary respite from death. Again there was a choosing by fate. One by one the exhausted men lost their hold and were swept off into the sea. About midnight, the mainmast gave way, and only ten regained the rigging. When morning broke there were only eight alive and all but two were so near dead with exhaustion as to be indifferent whether they were rescued or not. People on shore came down to the point opposite to where the ship sank and kept fires blazing all night. They were close enough to talk with those clinging to the wreck, but no effort was made at rescue.

26

Day came; the weary hours dragged on and still no attempt was made to save the perishing sailors. The Herring Cove men are not proud of their forbears' conduct; they would not do so today. The fact remains that nothing was done until about eleven o'clock on the morning of the 24th.

Then a boy, a mere child of thirteen, put off singlehanded in his skiff. He had to row down the cove, then out into a perfect witch's cauldron of breaking waves, recoil, eddy, and countercurrent. Every moment he was in deadly peril; every moment he was straining every muscle to the utmost. How he managed remains something of a miracle; but the fact is undoubted that he not only made head against that tremendous sea, but brought his skiff round and backed it in as near to the foretop as he dared. How eagerly his approach must have been watched by those eight drenched, numb, despairing men and with what alternations of hope and fear! The only two who can bear a hand are Dunlop and Monroe, and now they have a chance for life, surely they will take it. But that was not the mettle of the British tar in those great and gallant days. The two heroes on the wreck give up their last chance of life, and with infinite pains and difficulty fasten a rope round an insensible comrade, who only mutters a wish to be left to die in peace, and, as the boy brings his frail skiff alongside, they lower him into the little dancing ark of safety. This man is no other than John Galvin, master's mate, who bears a charmed life. When the *Tribune* sank he was below, directing the men at the chain-pumps. Washed up the hatchway into the waist, he was swept overboard, and sank, striking a rock. As he rose, three drowning men grappled him. He dived and they loosed their hold. He rose to the surface, clambered into the maintop, and seated himself on an armchest secured there.

About midnight, the mainmast fell and only ten of the forty clinging to it regained their hold. Now while he lies like a log in the bottom of the boat, a second man is lowered into it by the two great-hearted sailormen, and perilously overloaded, the "flat" starts for the cove. There is no risk to be run in returning, and wind and wave help instead of hindering the little boat. The men on the wreck strain their dull eyes after her until she disappears into the cove and safety. A long interval elapses. How long it must have seemed to the poor fellows clinging to their frail support above the waves! and how slight must have seemed the hope of rescue by a mere boy! At last the little boat with the single youthful oarsman in it appears once more at the opening of the cliff and slowly—very slowly, comes towards them. But the boy has overtaxed his strength. His hands are cramped on his paddles, the muscles of his arms and back are strained to starting;

in spite of his breathless labour, he shivers in his soaking jersey, and pull gallantly as he will, he can make no headway. The waves sweep him back; he grows weaker and weaker, and, at last, to save his life, he is forced to put about. But his defeat accomplished more than his success. The men were shamed into action by his glorious example of courage and determination. A volunteer crew was soon found for the jolly boat, in which four men had escaped the night before. Within another hour, the last survivor was safely landed. Only twelve men were left of a fine ship's company of nearly two-hundred fifty; among them, it is pleasant to find, were the two heroic sailors, Dunlop and Monroe.

That is the story of the *Tribune.* All this tragedy was played to its close at the harbour mouth between Thrum Cap and Herring Cove Head.

The shoal where she struck is called the Tribune Shoal to this day. Any fisherman or pilot will point it out to the curious, and, by laying the accent on the second syllable, prove the French origin of the word. As for the hero itself, little has been handed down. The rescued sailors could not say enough about his courage and his kindness. The great people of Halifax took him up, petted him, and showed their appreciation of his heroism by trying to make a gentleman of him. The Duke of Kent praised him publicly and got him a midshipman's berth on the flagship. But he pined under the restrictions of naval discipline and was allowed to return to his old way of life. Apparently he was a fisherman's apprentice, without kith or kin in Herring Cove. There is a tradition that he was weak in the head, which is not borne out by the skill and determination shown in the rescue. He must have been a simple soul. When asked by the royal duke in his princely way to name his own reward for his golden deed, he requested—says tradition—a pair of corduroy breeches! His name is not certainly known. Tradition says it was Joe Cracker, otherwise, Joseph Shortt. The Herring Cove fishermen remember his nickname and say that he went away to sea and was never heard of again. They believe that there is an accumulation of pension awaiting his heirs in England. They know well where the wreck lies, for their nets foul on the jagged timbers every now and then. The *Tribune's* dead are all buried in one field near where they perished. But for the dauntless fisher boy, like Browning's hero,

> Name and deed alike are lost,
> Not a pillar or a post
> In his Croisic keeps alive the feat as it befell.

The Yarmouth waterfront around the turn of the twentieth century

THE FIRST MATE

I

THE *REGINA* GOES

A life on the ocean wave has been the theme of many a joyous song, but life on board the lightship which is tethered head and tail over the "Lurcher" shoal near Yarmouth is, for green hands and wireless operators, one unending bout of seasickness. Hence a considerate Department of Marine and Fisheries allows the crew one month ashore out of every three. In one such period of shore leave, I caught Captain Nehemiah C. Larkin alone in his own house, with his coat off, filling in some government returns. These he courteously pushed aside to tell me his experience in the Yarmouth ship *Regina*.

Let no Biblical or Puritan associations with his Old Testament name mislead. It did not prevent him from being six feet tall, with a handsome, clean-shaven, ruddy face and laughing blue eyes—a typical sailor. Before his hair turned white he must have been as magnificent a piece of manhood as ever trod a deck or kept watch and trick. He told his tale sailor fashion, with detachment, quiet humour, and a wealth of precise detail.

He ran it o'er, at my request, even from his boyhood days. He first went to sea at sixteen in the brigantine *Premier*. After getting his mate's papers, he sailed as first officer in the *Tsernagora* under little Ned Hilton, who died in her hold trying to put out the fire at St. Nazaire. While master of the *Coipell* in the West India trade, he was wrecked.

"She floundered," he said briefly, "and we were all floating around, some one way and some another," which must have been good practice for his next shipwreck.

The *Regina* was a full-rigged ship of 1,212 tons, of Bay of Fundy spruce, built at Tusket in 1873 for the western ocean trade, to carry cotton, grain, and oil. She was named for the owner's pretty daughter, Regina. She carried a crew of eighteen officers and men, commanded by big, handsome Joe Bain of Yarmouth, a singing seaman with a rich bass voice, and N. C. Larkin as first mate. In November of 1883, she loaded at Philadelphia with barrel oil and cleared for London on the fifteenth day of the month.

As she was loading, a dispute of some importance arose between the captain and the owners. One of the deck beams near the main hatch needed to be replaced, but repairs cost money and all owners object to expense, on principle. The upshot was that the *Regina* put to sea with the old deck beam, and it proved to be the little rift within the lute, the weakest link in the chain. Once again, the kingdom was lost for a horseshoe nail. Captain Larkin was too loyal to his dead and gone owners to complain of this extra risk. The life of a sailor is all risk, and one more or less hardly counts in the day's work.

32

It was a bad time of the year, the winds were variable, contrary, and on St. Andrew's Day, late in the afternoon, the *Regina* was far south of her course, lying hove-to on the starboard tack under a single triangular piece of canvas, the main try-sail. Being hove-to means that the ship cannot sail, but is trying to save her life in the turmoil of the storm by keeping her bows to it.

Even so, in the hurricane, she was listed to leeward, and the boarding seas filled her deck. To relieve the vessel of this burden, the crew smashed some of the bulwarks to leeward and let the water pour off as fast as it poured on.

A little before midnight, the wind suddenly shifted to west-southwest, blowing with hurricane force. The effect was to run the ship right into the seas to leeward. It was as if two gigantic hands had seized the *Regina*, wrenching her in opposite directions to twist the fabric asunder. Such a conjuncture looks like the deliberate malice of nature. The lee seas tumbled in on her and swept the deck. Naturally, Captain Bain tried to get his ship before the wind. The foresail and the fore topmast staysail were set, but the vessel was lying over so far that she would not answer her helm. The foresheet was carried away and the sail was blown to ribbons; even the sails on the yards, though furled in the gaskets, were also flogged to pieces.

"We had to cut them away and tried to keep things together as much as we could," said Captain Larkin. "During the night the seas broke the hatch partitions and washed the tarpaulin off the hatch. We got a sail and put it over the hatch and battered it down to the deck as best we could, but it was torn away. We repaired it three times with the same success. Then, of course, she began to leak, and the men were set at the pumps. They were washed into the lee scuppers and were rescued with difficulty.

"It was after daylight the following morning, while all hands were at the pumps, she shipped a heavy sea from the weather or starboard side, carrying away the stanchions and bulwarks from the break of the poop to the forecastle head. It took the forward house off her, broke in the cabin skylight, and carried away the binnacle.

"The *Regina* was what we term a full poop ship; the poop extended from the cabin well forward to the main rigging. Four hundred barrels of oil were stored in it. The two boats rested one end on a sill built on the forward edge of the poop, and the other on a 'gallows.' They were right over the pumps.

"We were at the pumps when this heavy sea hit the ship. It brought down the boat gallows, letting the end of the boats drop to the deck over our heads and smashing the fiferail and the pumps. But none of us was hurt, to signify. The boat on the port side slid forward out of its lashings and was immediately smashed up with the other wreckage on the deck. The starboard boat held in the grit, and we succeeded in hauling it aft on the poop. Our largest boat was secured on the top of the forward house and it was lost when the house washed off. That left us with one boat only, the smallest we had."

So the progressive destruction of the good ship *Regina* went on. She was lying on her side, the waves sweeping over her, helpless, for the fury of the storm allowed no setting of sail, nor would she answer to her helm. She might right, if the masts were cut away, an expedient of extremity.

"The vessel was listed so heavily that it was useless to try to do anything with her, so the captain said to cut away."

"Cutting away" suggests to the landsman chopping down the masts as a lumberman fells a tree, but the process is much simpler. By slashing through the standing rigging, the shrouds and stays, on the side from which the strain comes, the masts break under their own weight. But all the axes had gone when that one wave cleared out the forward house, which is the carpenter's shop. How was the order to be obeyed?

"I had an axe in my room," said Captain Larkin, "which was kept in a becket on the bulkhead. I went down to get the axe and found the water about waist deep. The partitions were partly down; the one that had the axe had been washed out, and just as I stepped in the door, the handle lifted above the water.

"When I reached the deck, the captain said to cut the lines of the lower rigging, mizzen and main. The mizzen-mast broke at the deck and the mainmast, about twelve or fourteen feet above the deck. That carried away everything forward, except the lower foremast, which remained standing."

The three masts with all their load of spars had crashed over the lee side of the *Regina,* wrenching away the bowsprit and jibboom. All these heavy timbers, with their confusion of trailing cordage, were pounding at the side, but the stripped hull righted. Now, the trim *Regina* was definitely a wreck.

"We cleared away what wreckage we could. The wind began to moderate, but a heavy sea was running." There was a brief respite for the toilworn, fasting men. They had a moment to think of food and drink.

"The provisions and drinking water were all in a tank just aft of the pumps; and when everything smashed up around the deck, the vessel was full of water and burst up the hatches. The main hatch came off and the oil commenced to come out of the ship, and it spoiled everything. There was a small tank in the wash-room used by the captain, which we used to fill every morning. I asked him if there was any water in it, and he said he thought there was. I said I was going down for it.

"The cabin was partly full of water, and the partitions washing about. He thought a sea would board her any minute. Says he,

'If a sea caught you down there, you would never get out.'

"I told him I would put a rope round me and they could pull me out if I couldn't get out. Says he,

'You may get jammed among the wreckage down there.'

"I told him I would have to take that chance."

Be it noted that taking chances is the first mate's calling, and extra danger is his special perquisite.

"I succeeded in getting the water and a few biscuits that were below the waterline. That was all the water and provisions we had."

II

IN THE BOAT

On this, the first day of December, the elements relaxed for a little their persecution of the *Regina* and her crew. All hands were gathered aft on the poop of the dismantled hulk, while the captain and the mate drew apart and held council of war. Captain Bain thought that after so much bad weather, there would be a break in it, maybe a spell of fine weather. Though they were so far south as to be out of the regular traffic lanes from Philadelphia to London, yet if they took to the boat with what little water and provisions they had, they might succeed in getting far enough south to be outside the track of the North Atlantic gales. They stood a chance of being picked up by some vessel making a middling passage to the southward. Such was his argument.

Then the captain asked Larkin's opinion, for the first mate does not volunteer advice to his superior officer.

Larkin did not agree.

"I told him that as our boat was so small and the distance so far, and as we had no way of propelling the boat except by oars our progress would be very slow. I didn't think it feasible. I didn't think we could do it.

"He then turned to the men, and told them what his idea was, and also that I differed with him.

36

"'We can't navigate the ship anymore, and as soon as the oil comes out of her she must sink, as she has stone ballast in her. One man's life is as sweet as another's.'

"And he asked their opinion.

"They all decided with the captain. I said that I still held to my opinion but if they were all going to leave the ship, I wouldn't stay there alone.

"Later in the afternoon, we succeeded in getting away from the ship in the boat, with all hands in her and what little provisions we had, and started rowing to the southward, as best we could direct her. We hadn't a light of any kind. We found that our small boat was making a good deal of water, and with all hands in her, she was overloaded. While some were rowing, others were bailing. I expected to see her capsize at any moment."

So the boatload of castaways endured through the long, black December night, rowing, bailing, expecting every moment the final blow of fate.

"I remember asking the captain in the night if he could swim. He said he could. I said, 'If this boat turns over, let's get on the bottom of her. We'll take the last chance.'"

As uncertain, wintry daylight broke, the shipwrecked men made out a vague shape in the dim distance across the tumbling billows. It seemed a sail, to the north and east, more easterly than their own ship could possibly be, and hope of rescue sprang up in all their hearts. But that hope was soon dashed. As the light grew stronger and as they rowed towards the strange sail, they found it was the poor, abandoned *Regina*.

"The first remark the captain made was that we had better turn around and row to the southward—no use to go in that direction. The wind at this time began to air up again from a southwesterly direction. I suggested to the captain that we try to get back on board the wreck, as it would be impossible for our small boat to outlive any kind of a storm with so many men aboard. If we could get back on board, we could construct a raft that would give all hands a chance to save their lives."

This time, the mate's judgment prevailed. Captain Bain gave the necessary orders, and the boat got back alongside her mother ship.

"The ropes which we used in getting away from the ship were trailing over the side. The men got hold of them and hauled themselves on board. The boatswain stayed in one end of the boat and I in the other. We slipped two ropes under her keel, passed the ends over the side, and parbuckled the boat, and so succeeded in getting her on the poop again."

This means that being without davits or falls, the sailors passed ropes round the boat, made one end of each rope fast to bitts on the deck, and watching the favourable opportunity as the wreck rolled towards it, hauled on the free ropes and so pulled it on board by main strength. While the ropes were being passed, Larkin and the boatswain ran the risk of being swamped and the boat being smashed against the side of the wreck, but the post of danger is always the first mate's privilege.

BUILDING THE RAFT

"The captain and the carpenter started to fix up the boat as best they could. I took the others and started to construct a raft. We hadn't very much to work with. Our tools were all gone except the axe which was lying on the poop where we left it. For sills and the lower part of the raft we used the ship's spanker-gaff and boom. Then we cut the taffrail in sections, which ran round the poop. It was pinned down with iron stanchions an inch and a half thick. We had to cut those rods away with the same axe that we cut the rail off with. Not much of a cold chisel, but we did it.

"The raft was about fourteen feet by eight or nine. There was some small chain, old t'gallant sheets in a locker in the fo'c'sl' head. It would be a grand thing to secure the ends of the raft, which must be made solid if it was to stand the sea at all. If I could only get forward....

"The water was just washing over the main deck as it would over a ledge, but at times there was a lull. I took a coil of rope and made one end fast to a capstand on the poop. I watched my chance, and when the vessel lifted, I ran to the fo'c'sl' head with my rope and made it fast. This gave me something to hold onto and get what there was in the locker. Long before this, I had hauled off my sea-boots and oil-coat. I found I could get around quicker in my stocking feet. As I came back, a wave caught me, and the men yelled, 'The mate's gone, the mate's gone.'

"We got oil barrels out of the poop, emptied the oil out of them, plugged the bungholes, and lashed them securely, two abreast, to the lower sills of the raft and secured them thoroughly. For flooring we took plank which had been used for dunnage on top of the oil barrels. By evening, we had the raft completed, but we decided to remain on board until the morning."

The thoroughness of the job was tested by the unprejudiced winter storm. It stood the test; Larkin's lashings held and saved six lives.

"By night the wind was blowing a moderate gale, but by next morning it was blowing heavy, with a big sea running. Just at daybreak, the pins in the main deck came out of her. The whole forward part of the poop came out. While she had a heavy list to port, she took a heavier list, and fearing we would be all broken up with the wreckage, we decided to get away from her as quickly as we could. We launched our raft out and made it fast to the bitts on the port side.

"There was no decision made as to who were going in the boat or on the raft, but I had made up my mind that I was going on the raft. So I said, 'Those who are going on the raft had better come along,' so I started with two men besides myself. The ship was practically on her beam ends, and, at this moment, I heard the captain call, 'For goodness sake, somebody help us with the boat.' So I turned back to assist them.

"We tried to get the boat aft. In order to get her down between the skylight and the wheel, the stern had to be lifted off the bitts. But with the very heavy list of the ship, it was impossible to get a footing, and it was hard to lift her that high. While we were working with the boat, the wheel standard gave way, taking the wheel and all with it. That allowed the boat to run into the water.

"The captain was pretty well onto the forward part of the boat, and when she plunged into the water, it carried him along; he was holding onto the gunwale. A good many got into the boat, and I called to the boatswain, 'Get the captain in!' He, with another man, got him into the boat. He sang out to me, 'Come on!' I said I was not coming. 'You've got enough in the boat now.'

"They succeeded in getting out through the wreckage, oil barrels, spars, and so on. Just a mass of wreckage. I thought the boat would be swamped right there.

"When we first launched the raft, the boatswain, an Irishman from Dublin, grabbed the captain's big, black dog and threw him on the raft, saying, 'We may want your blood and meat before we're through with this job.'

"I looked round for the raft and found that when the vessel made her heavy list, it had carried the whole port side of the poop away and had taken the bitts which the raft was fast to. Consequently it had gone adrift and was quite a distance to the leeward of the ship. I thought it too far away for me to swim to fetch it, and I saw at that time but one man on the raft.

"I then scrambled up on the outside of the ship (which was the top part) into the mizzen-chains, and found that there were five men there who hadn't gone in the boat: the steward, cook, second mate, and two seamen. I said, 'I see only one man on the raft.' The steward said, 'The second man missed getting there. The raft pushed away. I saw him in the water and pointed to the raft. He shook his head and went out of sight.' That was the first man drowned.

"The captain backed his boat down to the raft and put out all the men but two. He kept two in the boat and made her fast to the raft. As the boat was the lighter of the two, he used the raft as a drag. The men with me made the remark, 'They're rowing back to get us,' but I told them it was impossible to row the boat to windward. We were all six lashed there in the mizzen-chains."

"Lashing" is not what landsmen and uninformed artists make of it. A sailor lashes himself to the mast, or, in this case, to the mizzen-chains, by fastening one end of a rope to something solid and slipping the other end, made into a loop, over his head and under one arm. This secures him from being washed away but leaves his arm and legs free. He can cut his lashing at any moment. Larkin and these five men were so lashed to the wreck, with the billows sweeping right over and half drowning them.

"The heavy seas were coming over the ship and would fairly tear you. Feeling confident the ship would go down in no great length of time, I looked about and saw a piece of the poop off the starboard side that the cabin was on, and I saw Mr. Dog on this piece of poop. He had jumped off the raft and swum back to the ship but could not get near her on account of the big wash of the ship. He had swum to that piece of poop and succeeded in crawling on top of it.

"I know I said to the men, 'While we are getting washed here, there is that dog standing on that cabin and there is not sea enough to wash him off. If another piece breaks off big enough I am on it.' Just a little after, I heard an extra crash, and looking up I saw the whole starboard side of the poop had gone away in one section. When it first broke, it rushed to the leeward of the ship, and when she lifted, I told the men, 'The whole side of the poop is gone. I am going on it.' When the vessel lifted, I ran along the side of her and jumping clear, swam down to the poop and got on it. The steward and one seaman saw me and also succeeded in getting on the poop.

41

"In a very short time, the ship being higher than this piece of poop, the wind drove her down so that we came back on the quarter. The three remaining men said that the vessel had lighted some; they had lengthened the ropes and had got away from the mizzen-chains and were protected from the wind. They thought they had a better place than the piece of poop I was on. They wanted to know if I was coming back. I said, 'No, she will go down.' We went out around the stern and the old *Regina* drove to the leeward of us. As night came on I could still see the ship afloat. The next morning nothing could be seen of her."

As the helpless *Regina* awaited her doom, her crew were in four divisions: the captain's dog on his own private piece of wreckage, the three men lashed to the sinking hull, the first mate with two companions on another portion of the disintegrating vessel, and Captain Bain with ten hands in the boat and on the raft. Let their part of the adventure be told next.

This is the situation.

The boat is made fast to the raft which serves as a drag to keep her head to the seas. There are three men with the captain in the boat and six on the eight-by-fourteen-foot raft.

About an hour after leaving the ship, the boat capsized, and all the provisions and water were lost. Captain Bain remembered what Larkin had said the night before about getting on the bottom of the boat. He dived out from under, got his hands on the keel, and by main strength rolled her over. The three men were still clinging to the thwarts. The men in the boat had taken hold of the painter and hauled the boat up to the raft and got on it. First they tried to haul the boat on top of the raft, but to put a twenty-four-foot boat on a eight-by-fourteen-foot raft was impossible. Next, they tried to bail the boat out. This they also found to be impossible. The boat and raft were smashing together, so they cut the boat adrift. Fifteen minutes later, the overloaded raft capsized in the stormy sea. Some of the men were lashed to it and were thrown underneath, but the whole of the eleven managed to get out from under and on the top of their frail refuge. The barrels were now uppermost and the level frame and platform below the surface. Those t'gallant-chains and scientific lashings of the first mate held fast. While the boat was afloat, the two drifted faster than the ship, but after it capsized, the ship drifted faster than the raft. Some strange sort of magnetism seemed to draw the *Regina* and the various fragments of her together. By evening, the raft was close to the wallowing hulk. The captain hailed the three seaman still on board and asked them where the mate was. They told him that he had gone off on a piece of wreckage and must have been drowned long ago. Desperate as were the chances of surviving on the *Regina,* it looked safer than staying with the raft. At least five of the hands thought so, after their two capsizings; as the raft neared the ship, they jumped for it and managed to get on board. The eight perished together that night when the *Regina* sank.

In the morning, the wreck was nowhere to be seen. "We were up to our knees all the time," was Captain Bain's report, "and continually drenched with the sea breaking over us. On the third day our sufferings were past describing. One man went mad and we had to lash him, so he could not get at the salt water. About noon on December 6th, we sighted a sail standing towards us. He passed us about two cable lengths off. He hove-to, clewed up all his sails except his lower topsails and mizzen-staysail, and lay for about half an hour, when he made sail and left us. It was hard to believe that a man calling himself a sailor could do such a thing, it being fine at the time.

"Another day and night we spent on the raft with every prospect of a gale from the southwest, but through the special providence of God, at noon next day we saw another sail standing for us, which came to us and hove-to. He put his boat out, though there was a strong breeze and heavy sea at the time, and came and got us. We were so weak they had to lift us off the raft and into the boat. We were taken on board the barque *Helen Finlayson* of Ardrossan, Captain Alexander Baker, and everything possible was done for us. It was to the kind and skilful treatment of the captain and his officers that we owe our lives, for we were very weak, and the least mistake might have proved fatal. By the time we arrived at Cork we were all quite recovered."

Though Captain Bain and the sailors lashed in the mizzen-chains of the wreck thought that Larkin was lost, he was still afloat on his fragment of deck. Like his captain, he had his eyes on his old ship as the December night gathered down, and, like him, the next morning he looked for her in vain. They could not have been far apart.

"The second night that we were on this raft," said Captain Larkin, "the steward said he couldn't stand it any longer. He was dying and didn't want to hold on any longer. The piece of poop we were on had broken off by a carlin almost as clean as if it had been sawed. There were the fife-rail and bitts at the foot of the mizzen-mast and part of the skylight. He said, 'I will sit down here and hold on to the stanchion as long as I can.' I said, 'I will tie you.' He said, 'No, I want to die,' and he soon washed away.

"The other man started drinking salt water, and he went out of his head. The first I knew of it he began asking how far we were from some place—sounded like Tron-yem. Then he said, 'What's the use of staying here starving? No use staying here. I was down there and saw the table spread. I looked in the window and there was everything on the table.' He said this in broken English; he was a foreigner. He said, 'Salt water don' taste too bad.' I said, 'You're not drinking salt water.' It was impossible to keep from drinking some, as we were under water part of the time. Then I thought I didn't know what he might do, so I reached round and took his knife out of his sheath. Before morning he had died. I was feeling pretty hungry but I said, 'I'm not going to eat you.' So I cut the lashing and let him go overboard. Then I was alone.

"Some time in that night or in the early morning, the wind moderated, so that if the boat was anywhere handy she could come to me. A little while after we drifted away from the ship, a white tablecloth floated out from underneath, and I grabbed it. The steward said, 'That's no good to keep you warm.' I told him the idea was that if there was a heavy rain we could catch the water and get a little to drink. On the second morning, I decided that if the boat was anywhere handy, they could come and get me. So I took the knife I got from the seaman and a belaying pin from the fife-rail, and with these tools I worked off a little of the moulding on the inside of the skylight. I lashed the strips together with some rope-yarn and attached the tablecloth to this flagpole and fastened it up on the bitt. I thought the boat might see it, if it was any ways handy. This raft of mine was not the best place in the world, and I wasn't anxious to stay there alone.

"Quite early in the forenoon, I sighted a sail to the westward. In a short time I could see that it was nearing me. Just how the sail was heading I couldn't tell until I got hold of the jibs. Then I saw the vessel was heading for me, or just a little north, most of the time. As she got near, I judged they also had bad weather, and everything was being broken up. I had the impression that everyone was busy. The mate would have his men at work, and I thought the chances of anyone seeing me would be pretty small. The captain might possibly be on the deck, and the man at the wheel might possibly be gazing around. So as the vessel came nearer, I got up on the bitt and raised the tablecloth in my hand to make it that much higher, and I held it up till the vessel was quite close to me. I could see men moving on the deck. By and by, they put the helm up, and I thought they saw me and that the captain intended to let his vessel come round to the wind and drop down alongside of me. When I saw that, I let my flag go, thinking it was no more good. At the last minute, the vessel hauled on her course again. I looked for my flag but as soon as it struck the piece of poop, it washed away.

"Then I wondered if it was possible to make anyone hear. I tried to sing out, but there didn't seem to be any power in my throat. Then I thought it might be eight o'clock and that they had shifted watch. But they had seen me, and the captain did what I thought at first he would do.

"When I was first discovered, it was eight o'clock, and the starboard watch had gone below. The vessel had double forecastles, the doors opening to the side of the vessel. They had all turned in but one man, and he was sitting in the doorway, smoking. The wind was on the quarter, blowing much harder than I thought. The vessel went down in a sea just as I happened to lift on one, and this man got the flutter of that tablecloth. He said, 'There is something down there with a white flag flying.' The steward looked and said, 'My, there is a man down there,' and ran aft to tell the captain. As soon as he came out on deck and glanced at me, he began to do what I had expected, that is, come up into the wind and drop down alongside of me. He put his glasses to his eyes, took a second look at me, saw the bitts, and thought there might be a whole hull there submerged. That was why he put the ship on her course again.

"His men were not in very good shape; they had malaria. It took him some little time to get volunteers and lower his boat. He got a little vial of water ready because he didn't know how long I had been floating around. He intended to give it to the men in the boat for me, but he must have been a little excited, for when he went up into the main-top to see where I was, and give the boat's crew directions, he forgot about the vial. As the boat came to me, I said, 'You can't come in there,' and I jumped in and swam to it. The boatswain, an old Welshman, in charge called, 'Don't throw your life away!' But I got alongside, and they picked me up. I was bareheaded, in my stocking-feet and shirt-sleeves.

"The vessel was the barque *Barroma,* Captain Hughes of Liverpool, England, loaded with cotton from Charleston, S.C. He was a kind and thoughtful man, as getting the vial of water showed. I told him about the *Regina* and the boat, probably to

46

the southeast of him, and he hunted round all day for them, but did not find them. We did see a wreck, Norwegian built, with no men on it.

"I was landed at Liverpool a little before Christmas."

The Arlington, *Yarmouth barque, under full sail*

A VISION OF THE NIGHT

In the year 1872, there was a barque of 542 tons built at Quebec, in Narcisse Rosa's yard, and christened the *Countess of Dufferin* out of compliment to the beautiful and gracious lady who came that year to Canada as the consort of our most popular Governor General. For nigh on twenty years this ship endured the sea, a long life for a wooden vessel, and this is the saga of her last voyage.

In the latter end of 1891, the *Dufferin* was loading lumber at Saint John, N.B., as many a vessel has done before and since. Her hold was packed with square timber, like a sausage with meat, and her deck was piled with fragrant spruce and pine deals, lashed, chained, and wedged together until they seemed part of the ship itself. Ship and cargo together must meet the ordeal of North Atlantic winter weather.

On December 15 she put out from Saint John for Londonderry. For ten days she met with variable winds and weather, but on Christmas Day, a southwesterly gale was helping her strongly on her road to Ireland. Captain Doble, however, noticed that the barometer stood at the ominous figure 28 and still was falling. Expecting "something heavy" he had his main topsail goose-winged, which means that half this sail on the weather side was tied up tight. So with just a rag of canvas showing, the ship was hove-to, facing her dangers.

Captain Doble also put out a sea-anchor or drag to aid in keeping his vessel head to wind.

The warning of the falling glass was soon fulfilled. Hardly was the *Dufferin* put in this posture of defence when, out of the north, another gale smote the barque with hurricane force, "accompanied by heavy cross-seas." The deep boiled like a witch's cauldron. Cross-seas are commingling, fighting billows, a confusion of contending, furious water-jotuns, trampling down the strongest ship and crushing it like a child's toy.

As soon as the tempest struck the *Dufferin*, it was plain to see that the huge deckload would put her down. It had to be jettisoned. All the hard labour of the Saint John stevedores had to be quickly undone by desperate men fighting for their lives. But they succeeded with great difficulty in getting the last stick overboard, which brought the labouring vessel some relief.

All Christmas Day, the *Dufferin* tried to hold her own, but manifold, sudden, terrific strains in all directions and the direct assaults of the sea began to dismember the luckless vessel. And the winter night closed down.

Before the bleak dawn of the next day, the combers that swept over her had smashed through the forward part of the cabin and carried overboard all provisions.

The crew managed to get two barrels of apples out of the stateroom, but before they could be secured, they were washed away. Most of the drinking water was in casks in the lower hold. The salt water got in and spoiled it. For six days following, the crew of the *Dufferin* had not a crumb to eat or a drop to drink.

The ceaseless buffeting and racking of the ocean sorely tried the old barque. The oakum started from every seam, and the water came pouring in. The pumps were manned, and the crew did their utmost to keep her free, but their labour was useless. Besides, the bitter wind covered the decks with ice. Pumping became too dangerous, and Doble, with the good captain's sense of responsibility for the lives of the crew, called his men off. The pumps ceased to clank, the water poured into the hull, and the

Dufferin settled down and down, till her deck, over which the waves washed ceaselessly, was flush with the sea.

It stands to reason that a vessel loaded to the hatches with wood is very like a solid log. Like a log, she may roll and pitch and wallow in the sea, but she can no more sink than a log. So it was with the helpless *Dufferin*. There was nothing more for the crew to do but hold on and not despair, while the drag still held her head to the sea, and the pitiful red ensign streamed from the rigging, union down. Starving, freezing, they crouched together under the slight shelter of the forecastle. The short winter day ended, the long winter night came on, and then the grey dawn. Then the final calamity showed its face.

The close-packed timber in the hull took up the water and began to swell. Something must give way and that something was the old frame of the doomed barque *Countess of Dufferin*. The men could see the deck bulging. It was only a question of hours when their ship would go to pieces under their feet in the chaos of billows. So passed Monday, the 27th, Tuesday, the 28th and Wednesday, the 29th of December, without a sign of rescue or the least alleviation of their sufferings. When would the end come?

Now the story turns eastward to Cardiff in Wales, where the Yarmouth barque *Arlington* of 849 tons is moored alongside the wharf. Her captain was Samuel Bancroft Davis also of Yarmouth, Nova Scotia, a lucky shipmaster who, in all his forty years at sea, never once had to wait for a fair wind. He was a "driver," once beating the steamer from Quebec to Havre in the barquentine *Peerless* with a load of deals. While at Cardiff the board of trade decided that the owners of the *Arlington* did not make sufficient provision for the safety of the crew and decreed that a new lifeboat of the latest build and pattern should be added to her equipment. Later, that boat proved its right to the name. The *Arlington* herself was not a lucky ship. First and last, she was the death of thirty-two men, but before the end, she had something to show on the credit side of the ledger.

In this same December, the *Arlington* had brought a cargo of deals across the Western Ocean and was homeward bound in ballast to New York, all well on board. During the night of the 28th Captain Davis had a remarkable dream. He heard someone calling from a ship in distress. So vivid was the vision that he sprang from his berth and ran on deck to see if all was well. Beyond the wild winter weather, all was well. There was no sign of a ship, no sound beyond the wind and waves. In the storm, the staunch *Arlington* was making a good run under reduced sail. So Captain Davis went below again.

But his vivid dream, if it were a dream, would not leave him. Two terms seemed to stand before his eyes and to ring in his ears:

"Latitude, fifty-two north. Longitude, twenty-one west."

He got out his chart and fixed this position. It was a day's sail away to the northward, far out of the track of steamers and sailing-ships. To hunt for a derelict there or thereabouts would mean a wide deviation from his course and most serious loss of time. It might be the wildest wild goose chase. Nonetheless, that cry for help was so real that this hard-bitten driver of a Yarmouth captain altered his course two points to make the *Arlington* cross the spot in the ocean where his dream told him the derelict was lying.

At breakfast he told his dream to the mate, James L. Hemeon, also a Yarmouth man: "I saw us taking the crew off a square-rigged vessel, like our own. And I saw you going in the boat to get them."

Hemeon did not, of course, remonstrate or criticize. Yarmouth captains maintained discipline, with the accent on the middle syllable. But privately he thought his captain had suddenly lost his wits. He remembered the tragedy of the *Esther Roy*. Putting the ship on a new course to hunt for a wreck in mid-winter all over the Western Ocean on the strength of a dream was sheer madness. If he still wanted proof, there was the circumstance of his going in the boat to the rescue. Rigid etiquette and ancient sea custom prescribe that duty to the second mate, like oversight of the sails and rigging. The first mate's place is on board. Mr. Hemeon remembered other cases of masters going mad—Charlie Armstrong shooting the men off the yards—and so on. Nonetheless he carried out the orders and all that day the *Arlington* ran on farther and farther north over an empty, angry sea. Every mile she ran took her farther from her port of destination.

So passed December 29. Ship routine continued unbroken from watch to watch. Nothing happened. Everyone on board knew of the "Old Man's" vagary, and everyone shared the first mate's opinion. At midnight, Captain Davis took on for the middle watch and paced, as usual, the weather side.

Suddenly, about three o'clock, in the pitchy darkness, the lookout spied a darker mass upon the sea and sung out just in time.

"Something on the lee bow. No lights up. Cannot make it out."

53

Captain Davis luffed up, properly indignant, for running without lights at night is a crime, and shouted through the speaking trumpet:

"What ship is that? Why haven't you your lights up?" The *Arlington* had just missed crashing into the stranger and no more.

Out of the dark came the answer: "Barque, *Countess of Dufferin*—water-logged—sinking—we have nothing to put up lights with—please stand by till morning and take us off."

Davis shouted back: "I'll stand by."

Five long hours passed, as the *Arlington* made short tacks keeping her eye on the derelict. By eight o'clock it was barely light enough for the sailors to see what they were doing. The *Arlington* came as near the *Dufferin* as she dared and spilled oil over the side to make some sort of "smooth." Davis called for volunteers, for a captain cannot order men to almost certain death, and three able seamen, all Irish, stepped forward: Daniel Keefe, Frank Sullivan, and Thomas O'Leary. Unknown to them, the crew of the derelict were mostly Irish. As they were launching the new lifeboat, the second mate, Anderson, was on the rail, busy with the falls, when a sudden roll of the ship jammed him between the boat and the davits. He broke three ribs and a bone in the right forearm. So the first mate, Hemeon, had to go in the boat after all.

It was no easy work launching her in that wild sea. Two trips were necessary to take off those eleven men from the *Dufferin*; the rescue occupied an hour and a half. Every moment had its own danger and difficulty, but the stout hearts won through. Before she could be got on board the *Arlington* again, the new board of trade lifeboat was smashed against her side, but it had served its predestined purpose.

Everything possible was done for the starving, frostbitten castaways. Food, medicine, clothing were given with sailor generosity. Captain Davis had forty pairs of woollen socks in his chest and he used them all. Captain Doble's feet were so badly frostbitten that he was in hospital in Baltimore for weeks. As soon as he reported his vessel abandoned at sea, latitude 52° 30' north, longitude 21° 20' west, to be exact, he wrote a grateful letter to his preserver.

On the representations of the British consul at Baltimore, where Doble told his story, the British government gave Captain Davis a fine gold hunting-case watch for his "humanity," while the board of trade presented Hemeon with a silver medal, and the three intrepid Irishmen with a bronze medal and three pounds sterling apiece for "gallantry in saving life at sea."

Captain Davis was accorded one more peep into the future, when the *Peerless* was being treated rudely at Glace Bay in the matter of loading coal. He dreamed that the steamer which unjustly was to have his berth, lost her propeller and could not get in, and also that the mine would take fire. He told the agents of both events before they happened, so they were only too glad to load "that d—d barquentine" and get her away.

As to the rescue of the *Countess of Dufferin*, Captain Davis offered no explanation and formed no theory. "He rather felt," said his proud son, "that the Almighty had used him to carry out His wishes."

Sketch of Captain John Stairs, London, 1842

JORDAN THE PIRATE

On the morning of September 13, 1809, a strange little craft called the *Three Sisters* was off Cape Canso heading for Halifax. She was a new fishing schooner of about sixty-four tons burden, tub-like in build, her beam being considerably more than the traditional one-third of her length, which was forty-five feet six inches from stem to stern. Besides her tubbiness, she had other noticeable peculiarities—a remarkably high stern and a very swift sheer, which means that, seen in profile, the line of her rail ran steeply down from the lofty poop to the bow. Not much money had been spent on the usual decorations of a vessel. She had no carved and painted figurehead, no gallery to her square stern, and no cabin windows; she had not even the usual wooden mouldings there. Instead, she bore mere bands of yellow paint on her black body. Another yellow streak ran fore and aft along her sides, and from the break of the quarterdeck forward of the mainmast, a band of white paint stretched to her stern. She was a noticeable craft. Her dumpy build, her colour scheme, her measurements, her lack of the usual marine adornments would make her easy to identify as far as a spyglass could reach.

Her cargo consisted of about six hundred quintals of dried cod. Four men were sufficient to handle her. John Stairs, master mariner, was in command. He belonged to a family which has been honourably connected with the commerce of Halifax for well-nigh a century and a half. There is fighting blood in the strain. Captain William Stairs was Stanley's right hand in the Emin Bey expedition and bequeathed the name to a peak in Ruwenzori. His brother commanded H Company of the Royal Canadian Regiment, which, on February 27, 1900, enfiladed Cronje's trench at Paardeburg and so forced him to raise the white flag. For this feat, Captain H. B. Stairs was enrolled in the Distinguished Service Order. When the Great War broke out, twelve youths of the name donned khaki; one Halifax church has mural tablets to six who never returned. The mother of this John Stairs died of the yellow fever plague in Philadelphia, and he was sent to Halifax to be brought up by his maternal grandfather. Like so many spirited boys, he ran away to sea and soon worked up to the rank of master. On this September day he had to fight for his life.

The mate was John Kelly, a black-haired soft-spoken young Irishman of twenty-three, about five feet six inches in height. His thin rather ruddy face was pitted with smallpox. The two hands were Benjamin Matthews, seaman, and Thomas Heath, a seaman and pilot, which meant in those days a man with local knowledge taken to assist in the navigation of a vessel in one voyage. Heath was a Halifax boy with a wife and two little children.

Besides her crew, the *Three Sisters* carried six passengers, namely, Edward Jordan, his wife Margaret, and their four children. The eldest was a boy of nine; the eldest of the three little girls was badly disfigured by burns on her arm and back. Like Kelly, Jordan was an Irishman; he was about thirty-eight years of age, with dark hair, dark eyes, large eyebrows, a ruddy complexion, and very white teeth. He is described as having a very black beard, which means that when he omitted to shave, the face hair came out thick and dark. To look at him you would not say that there was any harm in him. People noted that he had an innocent expression, but he had had a varied career before this eventful voyage in the vessel that once had been his own.

Born in the county of Carlow, he joined the rebels who were preparing for "Ninety-eight." In 1797 he was captured, tried, and sentenced to death for his share in the projected rebellion, and for the offence of drilling men by night. According to his own account, he saved the life of three persons the rebels were about to shoot. In some unexplained way he escaped from confinement, joined the rebels again, and was caught a second time. In 1798 he took advantage of the King's Pardon, married, and five years later he emigrated to America. Arriving in New York, he travelled to Montreal, thence to Quebec, and finally brought up at Gaspé. Here he got employment as a fisherman with a merchant of St. John's, Newfoundland, whom he served for five years. But bad luck pursued him. Other men prospered, but Ned Jordan seemed always to fail.

In June of 1808, he appeared first in Halifax and bought some goods from Jonathan and John Tremain, a prominent firm of merchants in those days. He was a stranger to them; they had never seen him before. No doubt he bought his goods, fisherman fashion, on credit.

In September of the same year he came again, asking for further credit, in order to complete and rig a schooner which he had on the stocks. Being prudent businessmen, the Tremains wanted security, and agreed to give him the credit he asked if he would make over his incompleted vessel to them on bill of sale; and this was done. Jordan mortgaged his unfinished schooner for supplies and goods.

Early in July of 1809, Jordan turned up again in Halifax with his new schooner, trying again to obtain supplies for himself and his family. In Halifax he was arrested for a small debt. This the Tremains paid and allowed him to go back to Gaspé in the *Three Sisters,* with Captain John Stairs in command. Jordan assured them that he had a thousand quintals or more of fish there, ready for shipment. Such a cargo would be more than enough to cover his debt to the firm.

At Percé, Captain Stairs found only about one hundred quintals of fish instead of the thousand Jordan promised. The bill of sale was regularly executed, and the *Three Sisters* passed lawfully into the possession of the Tremains. Captain Stairs picked up about five hundred more quintals of fish, and on September 10, started back for Halifax, giving Jordan and his family a free passage to that port. Nothing material happened in the three days' run down the coast to the Gut of Canso, but black murder was brewing on board the dumpy, yellow-streaked schooner with the high stem and quick sheer.

Shortly before noon on September 13, the *Three Sisters* was about three miles west of Cape Canso between that point and White Head, and four miles out to sea. This means that she was well clear of the land and that the master was shaping his course by the outer passage for Egg Island and Halifax Harbour. The wind was blowing strong offshore. Kelly the mate was at the tiller, and all the Jordan family were on the quarterdeck. Captain Stairs went below into the cabin to get a book out of his seachest, and then went forward to assist the crew with the sails. He returned to the cabin for his quadrant in order to take the sun at twelve o'clock precisely and so determine his position. Heath, his pilot, followed him down the ladder. He was turning over the leaves of the book, probably his Nautical Almanac, to get his declination, when a sudden shadow over the skylight made him look up, only to see black-faced Ned Jordan pointing a pistol at his head a few inches away. Stairs made an involuntary start, and at the same instant Jordan pulled trigger. The instinctive recoil from danger saved Captain Stairs's life. The bullet grazed his nose and cheek and lodged deep in Heath's chest. The poor fellow dropped to his knees crying, "My God! I am killed!"

One can easily picture the scene in the murky little cabin—the ear-splitting roar of the explosion within the narrow space—the acrid, choking smoke of black powder doubling the gloom—the mortally wounded man bleeding on the cabin floor—Captain Stairs probably prostrate also, but if not, stunned, blinded, deafened, with his face raw and burned. The situation he had to cope with would try the strongest nerves. The murderous assault came without the slightest warning. One moment he did not dream of danger; the next, death stared him in the face.

But the sailor's mind works quickly. His life is made up of instantaneous decisions. The safety of the ship and of all on board depends on prompt action. It took Captain Stairs but a few seconds "to recover from his fright and the effects of the powder," as he himself put it, but he soon pulled himself together. His first thought was weapons. He rushed to his sea-chest for his pistols. They had been there ten minutes before when he took out his Nautical Almanac, closed down the lid, and turned the key in the lock. In the brief interval his chest had been broken open and his pistols were gone. He rushed for his cutlass, which hung within easy reach, at the head of his berth. It was not there. He was unarmed, in a trap, but he would not meet his fate passively. In his own words, he "determined to go on deck." His portrait shows determination written in every line of his face. He was a shipmaster assaulted and braved in his own ship; he was an angry and an injured man; he "determined to go on deck." Over his head he heard several pistol shots, which he could not account for but which certainly meant danger. Jordan was shooting Matthews, the other sailor.

As Stairs began to run up the short cabin ladder, he met Jordan with his foot on the top rung, a cocked pistol in his right hand and an axe—the broad, heavy, short-hefted hatchet of the period—in his left. He was coming down to finish the job, but doubtless he thought that Stairs was dead and that he had to deal with Heath. With a cry to spare his life, Stairs fought his way to the deck and grappled with his would-be murderer. He seized Jordan's arms and pushed him backwards. Jordan thrust the pistol against his breast and pulled trigger, but the flint merely snapped on the steel. Stairs seized the pistol by the muzzle, wrenched it out of Jordan's hand, and flung it into the sea.

A wrestle for life and death ensued. On the tiny, uncertain quarterdeck, encumbered with the ship's gear and with Margaret Jordan and her children, the two men fought and struggled for the mastery. Stairs shouted to Kelly, his mate, to help him. Kelly, the traitor, made no answer, but remained at the tiller keeping the schooner full and by before the strong westerly breeze. Loyal Matthews, the other seaman, though desperately wounded, came staggering aft to his captain's assistance, but Jordan's bullets had gone home, and he collapsed bleeding profusely at Stairs's feet. In the swift-flying seconds, Stairs had managed to wrest the axe out of Jordan's grasp and tried to strike him with it, but now Jordan, in his turn, held his arms so that he could make no effective use of his weapon. In some way, Stairs succeeded in heaving or dropping it over the side, so that if it did not advantage him, it would not arm the man who was set on taking his life.

A second time Stairs called on his subordinate for help, but Kelly kept his place at the helm, turning his back, and in ominous silence, went on charging his pistol, apparently the first pistol which Jordan had emptied through the skylight. Now Margaret Jordan took part in the fray, crying:

"Is it Kelly you want? I'll give you Kelly!"

The Amazon caught up a boat-hook handle and struck Stairs several blows, without, however, doing much to disable him. He fought himself clear of both his assailants and rushed forward towards the bow of the schooner. He had time to notice Heath lying dead on the starboard side in a pool of blood. He had succeeded in crawling on deck, perhaps with the idea of aiding his captain, perhaps instinctively trying to get into the air. Mrs. Jordan had given him the final blows. Meanwhile Jordan had got hold of another axe and rushed forward after Stairs. Poor Matthews was in his way, lying where he had fallen on the deck, bleeding from his wounds. When he saw Jordan running amuck his thoughts were not for himself. With a sailor's loyalty, he cried:

"For God's sake, don't kill the captain!"

Jordan checked in his fury for a minute to smash in the head of Matthews with four or five blows of his axe. The brief pause gave Captain Stairs another chance. By this time he had made his way back to the quarterdeck. He was literally between the devil of murder and the deep sea. His two faithful men were lying dead on the deck. His treacherous mate was aiding and abetting his would-be murderer. He had no sort of weapon to his hand, and Jordan was making swiftly for him with his bloody axe. His back was to the wall. The seaman's life is made up of instantaneous decisions. In this desperate extremity, Stairs grasped at the one desperate chance for safety.

"Finding no chance of my life if I remained on board, and that I might as well be drowned as shot, I threw the hatch overboard, jumped in after it, and got on."

These words of Captain Stairs are perhaps not reported exactly. What happened was this. Driven into a corner, he seized the booby-hatch, the small sliding panel that closes the top of the cabin companionway, pulled it out of its grooves, and holding it in his hands, leaped over the taffrail into the sea. To trust his life to a little float of wood some two or three feet square offered the only possible way of escape, and it did not prove fallacious.

63

The whole struggle could only have taken a few minutes, probably not more than five or ten. One can easily picture the fierce struggle of two contorted figures on the quarterdeck, the four frightened little children, the virago of a wife striking viciously into the melée with her club, the prostrate bleeding sailors, the race of Stairs around the length of the pitching, rolling schooner, until he sprang over the taffrail with his improvised lifebuoy. And all the time soft-spoken John Kelly is at the tiller, keeping the schooner on her course. It is a strange scene.

Jordan's blood thirst was still unslaked, although his enemy had seemingly gone to certain death. He wanted to make sure by pistolling the man in the water, but Kelly dissuaded him, pointing out that Stairs was sure to drown so many miles from shore.

Jordan forbore to fire, but afterwards he had cause to regret his weakness. The *Three Sisters* bore away to the eastward with her living and her dead and left her late master a bobbing head among the waves. Not another sail was in sight, and the wind was blowing strong off shore. "Providentially" was a word in common use in those days. People believed in a Providence and saw the hand of God in the escape of Captain Stairs, for he was not destined to drown that September afternoon between Cape Canso and White Head. His time had not come. For three hours and a half he clung to the booby-hatch with the energy of a drowning man, and then, in his extremity, when he was "almost lifeless," he was picked up by the American fishing schooner *Eliza* of Hingham, Massachusetts, Levi Stoddard, master. To the minds of that day such an event did not seem to be the result of chance. It was arranged by an overruling power. At the very time his enemy thought he had accomplished his destruction, the rescuing vessel, though unseen, was on the way to save him.

Captain John Stairs must have been a strong man. Although almost lifeless when picked up, he was soon able to go on deck. He could see the *Three Sisters* a speck on the horizon, and he urged Captain Stoddard to alter his course and pursue the lost schooner. This Stoddard prudently refused to do, arguing that if damage ensued to his vessel in such an undertaking his owners would hold him responsible. Neither would he land Captain Stairs at Halifax, for the excellent reason that on his way down the coast his pilot had been impressed by the British cruiser *Bream*. When the *Eliza* was near the western end of Nova Scotia the wind was adverse, and Stairs could not be set ashore. He was carried as a passenger to Hingham. In a letter to the Tremains he writes that he will ever be indebted to the kindness and humanity of his rescuer.

As soon as possible, Captain Stairs made his way from Hingham to Boston and got into touch with the acting British consul there. This official promptly circulated a description of the *Three Sisters* and her crew to all collectors of customs, with instructions to arrest Jordan and Kelly on the charge of piracy and murder. These crimes excited great horror and indignation in Halifax, where Captain Stairs was so well known and respected. In a strongly worded proclamation, the governor offered a reward of a hundred pounds for the arrest of the murderer. These prompt measures soon brought Jordan within the grip of the law. He managed to navigate the *Three Sisters* as far as the Bay of Bulls in Newfoundland, which is near the capital St. John's. There he engaged Patrick Power, a fellow countryman, to take the schooner across the Atlantic to Ireland at eleven pounds a month until discharged. During the stay at Bay of Bulls there were quarrels between Jordan and his wife and drunken orgies on board the blood-stained schooner. Jordan had succeeded in obtaining the services of a navigator and was starting on his voyage when he was overhauled by His Majesty's schooner *Cuttle* and brought in irons, with his wife and children, to Halifax. Kelly had deserted his accomplice and remained on shore, but he was captured soon after by a detail of the Nova Scotia Regiment between Petty Harbour and Bay of Bulls. The Society of Merchants in St. John's gave Lieutenant Cartwright, who commanded the party, twenty guineas for capturing such a desperate character.

At Halifax, Jordan was given a most stately trial, for under the Acts of William and Mary, the court of admiralty convoked by special commission consisted of all the notables available. The president was the governor of the province, Sir George Prevost, who mishandled Wellington's veterans so shamefully at Plattsburg. Other members of the court were the admiral of the station, Sir John Borlase Warren, the chief justice, Sampson Salter Blowers, who lived to be a hundred and never wore an overcoat, His Majesty's council, and all the captains of His Majesty's ships which happened to be in port. It must have been a most imposing array, with every officer in full-dress uniform, and the judges in their official robes. Before the trial, Jordan and his wife were examined by a magistrate. They had concerted a flimsy tale with drink and jealousy as the leading motives. Of their accusations Stairs could have known nothing, but his evidence in the trial tore the tissue of lies to shreds.

Jordan's trial was brief. He was found guilty, condemned to death, and promptly hanged by the neck until he was dead, and then gibbeted at Black Rock, near Steele's Pond. The place is called Jordan's Bank to this day. There he dangled in chains in sight of all vessels coming in or passing out of the harbour, as a warning to evil-doers, until his skeleton fell apart. On the opposite side of the harbour, on Mauger's Beach, there hung at the same time six mutineers of HMS *Columbine,* a gruesome spectacle. When the *Saladin* pirates were on trial thirty-five years later, Jordan's skull was picked up from the ground and is now preserved in the provincial museum. Kelly was tried, convicted, and sentenced to death, but he was afterwards pardoned.

"His appearance on the trial was that of a simple, timid lad, and indicated nothing of the bravo," is the statement of an eyewitness. Jordan gave it as his opinion that Kelly was deranged and, until the time of his leaving the *Three Sisters,* he threatened "to put a bad end to himself." His conduct during the fight on board the schooner seems hardly rational. Perhaps he felt remorse and fear after the deed was done. Margaret Jordan and her four children were left dependent on the charity of Halifax, but very soon enough money was collected from the charitable to pay their passage back to Ireland.

The strange experience of Captain Stairs was long remembered in Halifax. He had three hair's breadth escapes from death on the same day—when Jordan's first bullet just grazed his cheek, when his second pistol missed fire, and when the *Eliza* came up just in the nick of time.

Jordan's crime is quite comprehensible. A luckless, ruined man, overwhelmed with debt, he took a sudden desperate resolve to recover possession of the vessel he once owned, by plain murder.

When he saw the *Three Sisters* standing away from Halifax, he made his decision. And he came within an ace of succeeding in his design. If Stairs had not started instinctively at the sight of danger, if Jordan had blown out the captain's brains instead of wounding Heath, it is more than probable that with Kelly's active or passive assistance he would have got back the *Three Sisters*. The two sailors would have been easier to dispose of than the master. In his confession he lied as valiantly as he had about his thousand quintals of fish, in order to save his wife and Kelly from the gallows. Jordan was a criminal, he had killed two men, and he richly deserved his fate—and yet he shared our common humanity. It is impossible to forget that he named his last tragic venture for his three little girls, and when he saw the *Cuttle* bearing down, "his uneasiness became excessive, and he said, 'The Lord have mercy on me! What will my poor children do!'"

Hedley and May MacDougall (née Cumming) at Yokohama, just after their marriage

THE WAVE

The casual visitor to South Maitland will hardly believe that deep-sea ships were once built there. On one side of the flat, grassy, high-walled, wooded dell are the station, the little white inn and a few houses with their backs to the hill. Behind, a steep road curves up to the house of "Squire" MacDougall. There is no water visible. But here W. P. Cameron built the full-rigged ship *Savona* of more than fifteen hundred tons, and he launched her without mishap on August 26, 1891. Deep, hidden, winding creeks fill at the Fundy spring tide and can float the largest keels out to the Shubenacadie, out to the Bay, out to the five oceans, and around the world.

The *Savona,* named for that city on the Gulf of Genoa which has the credit of inventing soap, was a bonny ship, one of the latest triumphs of the Nova Scotia naval architect. She represented the culmination of the shipbuilder's art at the very moment when steam was driving sail from the sea. Above her royals, she carried sky-sails on her towering masts which seemed to rake the blue. Under full sail she was a picture to delight a seaman's eye, and she was as staunch as she was beautiful. That was shown when the test came, but, like other beauties, she was dogged by ill luck, until her final wreck. The captain's wife matched the ship.

One of "Squire" MacDougall's nephews was christened Hedley Vicars, like other Nova Scotia babies, in memory of that evangelical British officer who was converted while in garrison at Halifax and who died before Sebastopol. Hedley MacDougall went across the water for his bride, to Onslow, that lovely countryside, where the shire town might have been instead of Truro. The only daughter of Noble Cumming, justice of the peace, elder in the Presbyterian church, was a notable beauty. Blackhaired, rosy-cheeked, generous, loving to rove the world, twenty years of age, she was just the wife for a sailor. Even now, when her black hair has turned grey, May MacDougall would be singled out for her looks in any assemblage of women. A photograph taken in Yokohama shows her as a bride in Japanese costume, obi and kimono, seated on the floor pouring tea for her husband, who is also masquerading as a Japanese. The face is full of charm, at once fresh, fine, delicate, and strong: the broad forehead, the well opened eyes with arched eyebrows, the straight nose and firm chin testify to keen sensibility blended with vivacity and swift intelligence. It is Mimosa San in person, with the animation of the West.

So, she sailed with her husband in the *Savona* around the world. Her last voyage began on March 3, 1901, when the *Savona* was off the Falkland Islands; the captain and his wife were on deck together at the hour of sunset. The sun had sunk below the skyline, but the horizon was a broad band of ghastly green, in which were reflected many suns. It was a strange sight, a portent. Who could read the meaning of that sign in the sky?

The woman shivered, but not with cold.

"I don't like it," she said, within the strong arm that steadied her on the uncertain deck.

"Pshaw!" laughed the man. "Pretending to have nerves—*you!*"

But it was the last time he was ever to look on the sunset.

The last night of his life, Hedley MacDougall spent chiefly on deck. Harry Mosher, the second mate, a boy from Cheverie, had suffered much from a felon on his finger. The captain relieved him, for the junior officer might fall asleep from sheer weariness and endanger the ship.

About six o'clock in the morning, the sea became strangely agitated, pitching and tossing the *Savona* in an unaccountable manner. There was no storm, in the sailor's sense. Just the regular squally April weather off the Falklands. But the squalls must have been heavy, for two men, Victor Rosenkran, a Norwegian, and Karl Jensen, a Dane, were needed at the wheel to keep the big ship steady on her course. One squall fiercer than the rest carried away the fore topmast. The mild sea term means far more than one would think. A mast is built in three sections, the lower mast, the topmast, and the top-gallant mast, all joined together and held in place with the utmost of the rigger's art. The *Savona*'s topmast being broken, down it came with the top-gallant mast and the five yards they carried, crashing to the deck or over the side. The fall of the topmast brought down all the head-sails, the jibs and staysails rigged from the foremast to the bowsprit. Carrying away the fore topmast meant wreck to the forward part of the *Savona*. Her bow would be a tangled confusion of spars, sails, and cordage. For the time she was disabled and would not be herself again until the wreckage could be cleared away and new masts rigged. She was a cripple, like a man with a broken arm before it can be set.

About seven, the captain came down to the cabin for his morning coffee, and he had it in his stateroom with Mrs. MacDougall. He advised her to keep her berth on account of the rough weather. Nova Scotian captains were always slow to admit to their wives that a storm was raging. Then he went back on deck. Frank Johnson, the old black steward was setting the table for breakfast in the mess room. On deck all hands were busy about the forward deck, clearing the raffle and making such repairs as were possible under the direction of the first mate, John S. Kyffin of St. John; the captain was at his usual station on the house, ruling over all, when the *Savona* was pooped.

The landsman thinks of waves as the short ripples seen in marine pictures or as observed on his summer holidays by the seaside. Only the sailor knows that "mountain wave" is hardly an exaggeration. The wave is not a wave to the ordinary imagination. It is the sea itself, rising, lifting, and falling like a slipping hillside on the ship. Such a wave, doubtless of volcanic origin, unheralded, immeasurable, towering, had fallen on the ill-starred *Savona,* when she was all a wreck forward, overwhelming, drowning her.

A ship is built to take the blows of the sea in front. With its sharpness, its subtle curves, and its arch-like strength of structure, the bow is well designed to sustain the mighty buffets of the sea. The bow is at once a sword to divide and a shield to ward. But sometimes, in rare circumstances, the sea bludgeons the ship from behind, where, from her very nature, she is least fitted to endure the assault. The sea boards the vessel from the stem, or poop, with dire effect. Such a calamity had befallen the crippled *Savona.*

There was a crash like the crash of doom. The men forward saw the wave, seemingly forty feet high, curling over their heads, and they jumped for the rigging. The enormous billow struck and covered the whole ship many feet deep. She seemed sinking to the bottom. Well for the *Savona* she was buoyant wood and built of honest Bay of Fundy spruce. A ship of steel or iron with a cargo of stone would have sunk like a stone. But the stricken *Savona* slowly recovered and struggled to the surface again.

That single mighty blow wrecked the after part of the vessel and took four lives. It smashed the binnacle and the wheel. It killed the two men steering. They were found far forward, about amidships, and on the opposite sides of the deck, stone dead, under a pile of wreckage. Fastened to the bulkhead above the bureau in the captain's stateroom were three chronometers. One was found under the lifeless body of each wheelsman.

The strong-built cabin was swept clean. A battering ram of water drove straight through it, cutting out both ends, as neatly as carpenters could have done it with sharp axes, but leaving the roof and sides uninjured. The skylight was not even stove in nor was the glass in it broken. And yet the half-deck, the narrow alleyway which runs around the cabin on three sides, was crushed flat to the main deck below. The whole structure of the cabin was lifted slightly from its strong foundation on the transverse beams. There was a lateral thrust in this wave and also a tremendous downward blow, as of a supernatural trip-hammer, or piledriver.

In her berth, May MacDougall heard the crash of the falling cataract above her head and the splitting, cracking uproar of rending woodwork and found herself drowning under an icy flood. She was swept out of her berth with her mattress under her, through the bulkhead, or partition, which divided the stateroom from the saloon, through the partition that divided the saloon from the mess room, and through the farther end of the cabin. She brought up at the foot of the mizzen-mast under six feet of piled wreckage, cabin furniture, and splintered woodwork. The icy flood drained away swiftly. Chilled, choking, terrified, she heard Kyffin shouting orders, and she knew the captain was gone. Beside her lay the body of the black steward with every bone in him broken.

"I could have put out my hand from where I lay and touched him," she said.

Her only hurt was a little bruise on the right elbow. The lazarette and the breadbox behind the bed took the first shock of the terrific blow, and a heavy settee fastened to the saloon bulkhead had turned over her lengthwise and fended off the murderous wreckage. Her life was saved as by a miracle.

Captain MacDougall was nowhere to be seen. Just before the mountain wave broke, the mate had a glimpse of him standing on the top of the house. All thought he must have been washed overboard. There was no trace of him. But all the while he was not far away.

Fore and aft, the *Savona* was a wreck: "nothing better than an open boat from the stern to the waist." The wave had smashed the steering wheel; that meant the rudder could not be moved to guide the vessel through the world of waters. It smashed the binnacle, the thickset stand in front of the wheel holding the compass by which the helmsman steers; that meant direction was lost. The ship was afloat, her hull was sound, but fore and aft she was a wreck and lay a helpless log upon the sea that still buffeted and shook her. The storm raged with great fury for a whole week, during which time all suffered from want of food and clothing.

Kyffin proved himself the man for the emergency, as was the way with Bluenose mates. Out of a spare sky-mast he made a tiller and lashed it to the rudderhead, through which he fitted two crowbars. By means of tackles rigged to the bulwarks, the ship could now be steered by the simple process of pulling and hauling. This job was done in four hours after the accident, and it was a marvel to the old hands who saw the contrivance in port. The want of a compass was a harder matter. Two compasses had been damaged past repair, but a "tell-tale" compass escaped destruction. A tell-tale is an inverted compass hung face downward from the cabin ceiling so that the captain can see, without going on deck, if his ship is being kept on her course. The *Savona*'s tell-tale was found among the wreckage. The officers were not familiar with it and, to the nerve-shaken men, it seemed to have been thrown out of gear by the tremendous upheaval, like everything else on board. According to it, the sun was rising in the west. They brought the puzzle at last to the captain's new-made widow. The woman's wit suggested turning it upside down, when the sun came back at once to his proper station in the sky. So, the crew were able to make repairs and rig jury-masts.

The cook was an old Frenchman who suffered from rheumatism. Captain MacDougall had had the carpenter build a bunk for him in the galley, where he could keep himself warm.

Now, with the total destruction of his cabin, this became May MacDougall's quarters, and the cook berthed forward.

Without chronometers, without a proper compass, with a broken, patched quadrant, encountering frequent gales, still, Kyffin made the land in as true a position as steamers coming into port, fitted with the best of instruments. He was a sailor and the son of a sailor. Bringing the crippled *Savona* into port was a triumph of navigation.

Food was not a problem. There were canned goods, and the flour was not all spoiled. Water was a more serious matter, but it lasted to the voyage end, though it turned bad the day after.

In her crippled state, the *Savona* was twenty-six days in reaching Montevideo. She was once within sixty miles of port, when a *pampero* drove her off the coast, and it took eight days to recover the lost distance.

Some time after the accident, the cat which had been the captain's pet began to behave in a strange way, mewing and trying to attract the attention of the men. At last, on the eighth day, when the storm had somewhat subsided, they followed her. She led them to the wreckage still piled forward and under it was the dead captain.

"When the men found my husband, he was lying with his arms folded," said Mrs. MacDougall, as she told the story by her own quiet fireside, "and a tiny blue mark on his temple—no other mark or disfigurement. Death must have been instantaneous. As the big wave rolled up astern, the mate turned from his position on the forward deck and saw the captain standing on the top of the house. I always think he thought it was death for all and folded his arms to meet it."

Dispatch box saved from schooner Industry, *1868*

VIA LONDON

Nova Scotia has need of another Hakluyt to record the traffics and discoveries, the disasters and the heroic deeds of the seafaring provincials. For more than a century Nova Scotian keels ploughed the seven seas in peace and war. Five thousand vessels, Howe boasted, had been built in the province, and they carried the flag to every port in the world. Once Nova Scotia had even a tiny navy of her own. Privateering in three wars, mutinies, encounters with pirates, dreary wrecks, incredible endurance, rescues from death and destruction, crowd the record with moving incident. Many are the tragedies of the sea. What the ordinary perils of navigation may mean, what suffering seafaring folk may be called to undergo, with what hearts they met their trials will be plain from this simple tale of a little Nova Scotian coasting vessel. Because of the vessel's irregular course, the tale has been entitled "Via London," but perhaps a better name would be "Angeline's Wedding Dress."

At seven o'clock on the morning of December 11, 1868, in the dim dawning of a winter's day, the schooner *Industry,* thirty-seven tons register, put out from the wharf behind Ronald Currie's store on the west bank of the beautiful LaHave River. Below hatches she had stowed a cargo of dry and pickled fish, and on deck she carried a load of cordwood for the Halifax market. Lewis Sponagle was captain; with Currie he was joint owner of vessel and lading. Three hands were sufficient for the needs of the small schooner: their names were Henry Legag, Henry

Wolfe, and Daniel Wambach. Besides, she carried two passengers, Lawrence Murphy of Lawrencetown, and a young girl belonging to LaHave called Angeline Publicover, eighteen years of age, who was going to Halifax to buy her wedding dress. Her pictures shows her to have been small and slight in figure, and fair in the face, with candid brown eyes, brown abundant hair, rosy cheeks, and kind smiling lips. It is a fine face. She would have made a comely bride. She could have had no forewarning of the many trials she was so soon called on to endure, nor could she have dreamed that she would prove a heroine in a dreadful extremity.

The day was cold with light westerly winds which drove the *Industry* towards her port of destination, only fifty-four miles away. Perhaps no one remembered that Friday is not counted a lucky day for beginning a voyage. It was certainly ominous for the *Industry* and all on board. Using the earliest hours of daylight, she pushed out past Ironbound straight along the chord of the great double fold in the coastline made by Mahone and St. Margaret's Bays. In spite of the favourable wind, it was not a good sailing day. The westerly breeze was fickle, and the mild weather was merely the lull before the coming storm. It took the little schooner nearly seventeen hours to cover some forty miles, which means that she must have dawdled because the wind failed her. The short winter day passed; the black December night came on. The weather changed and with it, the fortunes of all on board the *Industry.*

About one o'clock in the morning of Saturday, December 12, they could see the light on Sambro Island, which for a century and more has been the beacon for all vessels approaching Halifax from the westward or the south. The light bore north-northeast. The deceitful west wind which had so far favoured them now died away, and suddenly, with the very slightest warning, the storm swooped down upon them from the northeast, bringing the blinding snow with it and hiding the dim loomings of

78

the land. Halifax Harbour is beset with dangers. It is a wicked coast to beat up to in a black winter storm. Progress towards the port was impossible, so the helm was put over, and the *Industry* turned in her tracks to run for LaHave. She went back faster than she came.

The veering of the wind must have been terribly sudden. Apparently the schooner was taken aback, for the first blast of the snowstorm split the foresail and made it useless. Henceforth the *Industry* was like a bird with one broken wing. This was only the first of the mishaps which befell the ill-starred vessel that dark night. At the same time the can of kerosene was spilled; the cabin lamp was never lit again, and it was no slight aggravation of their misery that more than half of every twenty-four hours must be spent in utter darkness.

In the double darkness of night and the thick driving snow, the *Industry* fled back to LaHave before the northeast gale. It was still thick weather when Captain Sponagle judged that he was near Cross Island, the seamark sentinel before Lunenburg harbour, to which Lunenburg sailormen find their way back from the ends of the four oceans. The mouth of the LaHave is just around the corner. Now the *Industry* was near home and safety, but once more her luck changed for the worse. The fierce gale suddenly chopped round to the northwest, driving the schooner back from her desired haven and out into the furious Atlantic. If her foresail had been intact, she might have been hove-to, and so have ridden out the gale. In attempting to do so, the damaged sail was blown to rags. There was nothing for it but to dowse all sail and run before the storm. For three days and three nights the *Industry* scudded under bare poles straight out to sea. To take the dangerous weight off her, the deckload of cordwood was started overboard. In the darkness and confusion all available hands must have been working desperately to clear the deck. They were fighting for their lives, and in their haste another accident occurred. One of the two water-casks secured just forward of the mainmast went overboard with the cordwood, and the other was so badly smashed that only two gallons of water was saved from it. This loss meant later intense suffering from thirst. The two gallons from the broken cask, and a kettleful of melted hailstones gathered in a remnant of the foresail, was the whole water supply of seven persons for eighteen days. They were rationed to a wineglass apiece once in twenty-four hours. The last drop was finished on December 27. Along with the deckload went their only boat.

Never counting on more than the day's run to Halifax, the owners had not provisioned their little craft for such an unforeseen emergency as being blown out to sea. Food there was practically none. What little they had was spoiled by the salt water. For two weeks, from December 15th to 29th, those seven persons sustained life on ten hardtack. A tiny fragment of biscuit once in the twenty-four hours was the ration. On that and the thimbleful of water, they kept the life in their bodies for an endless fortnight. They dared not touch the salt fish in the hold, for fear of the thirst that would drive them mad. With fresh water they might have been able to cook the fish, though the stove was damaged in the hurly-burly of the first night. They found a few oats in a bag, and these they managed to parch on the top of the broken stove and eat. On Christmas Day they discovered one potato in the bilge. They divided it into seven portions, just and loyal in their misery.

"Our tongues were so swollen we could scarcely eat it."

On Tuesday, December 15 they were able to do something besides hold on for dear life, as their frail little fabric raced the mountainous seas. In the turmoil of waters they saw another sail, an American fishing schooner, which ran down close enough to speak with the helpless *Industry*. The weather was too wild for the Americans to launch a boat with food and water or to render any assistance whatever. For a few moments the two craft were near enough for Captain Sponagle to shout that he wanted

80

his position and his course for Bermuda and for the American skipper to shout back the necessary directions; then each went his way. Once more the crew got some canvas on the *Industry*, the jib and mainsail, both close-reefed no doubt, and, starving and parched with thirst, they held on for the Summer Islands. The gale was favourable, but they were not destined to reach the port they were headed for any more than Halifax. Tuesday was evidently their first breathing space. On this day Captain Sponagle took stock, collected his ten biscuits, and began rationing them out, as well as the precious two gallons of water. For three days the *Industry* held her course towards Bermuda, but the faint gleam of good fortune, the hope of reaching port, proved to be illusory.

Once more the cruel wind chopped round to the westward and blew a terrific gale. Evidently the little schooner was buffeted by a series of cyclonic storms. December 1868 was a particularly bad month all over the North Atlantic. Many were the wrecks and reports of disaster. Like the former, this gale lasted three days, "during which," says the original narrative, "we suffered severely." The severity of their sufferings is easy to realize. This last gale was the worst of all, and it grew wilder and wilder. The huge confused billows made a clean breach over the labouring schooner, tearing away her bulwarks, rails, and stanchions, and flooding the tiny cabin. The force of the waves also wrenched the tarpaulin off the forward hatch and carried it away. To prevent the hold from being flooded and the vessel foundering there and then, the resourceful crew nailed over the hatch a cowhide intended for the Halifax market, and it kept the water out. But with the prolonged and furious buffetings of wind and sea, the frame of the *Industry* was being racked apart, the seams opened, and she began to leak badly. To the sufferings from cold, hunger, thirst, was added the exhausting, endless labour of pumping to keep afloat.

"Our strength was fast failing, but we managed by dint of great exertion to pump the vessel."

To strain every muscle of arms and back at working a machine which hardly forces the water out as fast as it runs in and to know that your life depends upon your perseverance, is the toil of Sisyphus. If the water rose in the hold beyond a certain point, the vessel's reserve buoyancy would be gone, and under the next swamping billow, she would go down like a stone. So these men laboured, hour after hour, day and night, on the reeling, wave-swept deck, toiling like slaves, with a few crumbs of biscuit, and a wineglass of water to sustain their strengths.

Christmas Day, with its happy memories, brought increase of misery to all on board the *Industry*. Their Christmas dinner was the solitary raw potato divided into seven portions, which they could scarcely eat. Christmas night was remembered for its terrors; it was a night of despair. Work at the pump was abandoned as useless. There was no one at the tiller; hope was gone. All seven were huddled together in the inky darkness of the little cabin. Overhead tons of water crashed upon the roof as the unguided *Industry* pitched and rolled and wallowed in the giant billows. There was nothing to do but hold on and wait for the inevitable end. The schooner might go down at any moment.

What was done in that cabin is best told in the words of a survivor:

"We were nearly exhausted with hunger and exposure and our thirst was dreadful, and expecting every moment to be our last we united in prayer to the Almighty and shook hands with each other, as we thought, for the last time. Most of the men gave way to tears, but our only female passenger cheered us with the hope that our prayers were answered, and we were strengthened again to pump the ship."

"Extremity is the trier of spirits," says Shakespeare. "Hope," says Chesterton wisely, "is the power of being cheerful in circumstances which we know to be desperate....The virtue of hope exists only in earthquake and eclipse….For practical purposes it is at the hopeless moment that we require the hopeful man…. Exactly at the instant when hope ceases to be reasonable it begins to be useful."

These words fit the situation to a nicety. It is no wonder that men weakened by a fortnight of exposure, starvation, thirst, and exhausting labour should shed hysterical tears, nor is it their shame. But the spirit of the female passenger did not break or bend. In the black darkness of that little cabin, the courage and hope of a mere girl shone like a star. Angeline Publicover cheered the despairing men by her faith in the mercy of God, and they were strengthened to resume their Sisyphean labours. On board the *Industry* the last morsel of food was eaten, the last drop of water drunk, when rescue came. All these weary days driving hither and thither in mid-Atlantic, another vessel was sailing to cross her track. The predestined meeting came to pass on December 29.

The Coalfleets of Hantsport were a typical family of Nova Scotia mariners. Once a nameless baby drifted ashore from the wreckage of a collier on the coast. The boy lived, and from these circumstances was given the name Coalfleet, meet origin for a seafaring clan. From him was descended Hiram Coalfleet, one of six brothers, all of whom followed the sea. He was a master mariner, honourable, looked up to, and a skilful navigator. In command of the Nova Scotia barque *Providence* of four hundred and eighty tons, he was now on his way from Philadelphia to London with a cargo of kerosene. His brother Abel sailed with him as chief mate.

His vessel got her name in a curious way. She was built in the beautiful little town of Canning by the well-known firm of Bigelow. When she stood almost complete on the ways with a little schooner beside her, the master builder decided that as the timbers were ready, the schooner should be launched that day. So it was done, and she floated safely into the narrow tidal river Pereau. That very afternoon a fire broke out which swept the whole village, but it stopped short at the barque's hull; the flames scorched her sides. If the schooner had remained on the ways, both vessels must have been burned. Hence the schooner was christened *Escape* and the barque *Providence*. Now the *Providence* was to earn her name a second time.

Seven hundred miles east of Nova Scotia, she sighted a vessel, as the expressive language of the sea puts it, "in distress." That so small a craft should be so far from land implied accident, and the wave-swept deck and the jagged fragments of bulwarks would tell their own tale. The *Providence* bore down on the schooner under storm canvas, lay-to, and tried to launch her longboat. It was still blowing a gale with a heavy sea running, and getting the big heavy boat over the side into the sea was no easy task. After several attempts, it was smashed and lost. The only other boat on board was too small to live in such a sea. But Captain Coalfleet was not at the end of his resources. He tried another means of rescue which put his own ship in peril, which called for most skilful handling of her, and which would fail but for cool, swift, decisive action. He manoeuvred his big barque to windward of the little coaster, backed his topsail, and drifted down on the *Industry* broadside on. He must have calculated his distance to a nicety, and he must have had a well-disciplined crew; no lubbers or wharf-rats stood by the sheets and braces that December day. He was risking his own ship with all on board, for collision was inevitable; his part was to minimize the shock of contact. As the two vessels swung crashing together, the mainyard of the *Providence* fouled the rigging of the *Industry*. Nimble as a cat, Abel Coalfleet ran upon the mainyard, lay out along it, and, with a line in his hand, probably the clue-garnet, let himself down swiftly on the tossing deck of the schooner. Any passenger on an ocean steamer who has ever watched the antics of the pilot's boat alongside in comparatively smooth water, can form some conception of the way two vessels rolling, tossing, pitching, grinding together would behave in a mid-winter Atlantic storm. Abel Coalfleet, balancing on the yardarm, which pointed in the sky one moment and the next almost dipped in the waves, makes the acrobatics of the circus and moving pictures look silly. He must have been as cool-headed as he was brave and strong and nimble. He might have lost his hold and been flung into the sea or entangled in the cordage or crushed between the grinding hulls. As he dropped to the reeling, wave-swept schooner's deck, he fastened a line to the one woman on board, who was speedily hauled up the side of the *Providence.* The six men were also swiftly pulled on board by means of ropes the crew flung to them, with Abel Coalfleet always aiding. Then he slashed the stay which held the yardarm of the *Providence* fettered, and swarmed up the barque's side like the people he had saved; the backed topsail swung around promptly, and the *Providence,* having sustained much damage, was once more put on her course for London. The rescue could only have taken a few minutes; it was effected "most expeditiously" say the rescued, in a smart and seaman-like manner. The collision gave the *coup de grâce* to the battered little coaster. Three-quarters of an hour later, she disappeared beneath the stormy Atlantic with her cargo of dry and pickled fish, her broken stove, and the cowskin on the fore-hatch. The *Providence* had come up just in time.

85

Of course, saving life at sea is more or less a habit with sailors, all in the day's work, and nothing to call for remark. A dry, matter-of-fact entry in the log of the *Providence* would close the incident. But this rescue was exceptionally hazardous and brilliant. The skill of Captain Hiram in handling his big ship was equalled by the way Abel seconded him. Sponagle, with a sailor's appreciation, records that he "gallantly hazarded his life to save ours." Gallant is the word.

The rescued seven considered their preservation while in the *Industry* "perfectly miraculous, and the manner in which we were relieved almost as wonderful." But they were in the last stages of exhaustion, with bodies wasted by nearly three weeks of starvation, and with tongues so swollen that they could hardly speak. All on board were most kind to the castaways, but they still had many hardships to undergo. Their proper place was a hospital ward with careful nursing and nutritious food until their sorely tried bodies recovered their tone. But the resources of a Nova Scotian barque in the sixties were limited; she would carry only coarse food to meet the bare necessities. Moreover the taste of kerosene had got into the food and water and produced painful sickness. It was not until three weeks after their rescue, on January 20, 1869, that they reached London, weak, utterly destitute, but thankful to God for His mercy that they were alive.

From London they were forwarded to Liverpool by kind friends, whence they returned to Halifax by the Inman Line steamer *Etna*. Angeline Publicover was particularly well treated by the ladies on board, who dressed her "like a queen." So at length they reached the port they set out for on February 12 in a varied and circuitous passage of sixty-one days. The newly organized Dominion of Canada paid the travelling expenses of these shipwrecked Nova Scotians. The Halifax papers showed no interest in the event; they did not interview the castaways, print their story or their pictures. Such adventures and exploits were too common. The shipping news occupied but small space in the local journals and is to be found under the heading "Reports, Disasters, etc." The "etc." is eloquent. In the sixties was the heyday of Nova Scotian shipping. The great industry of the province was reaching its peak of prosperity. So six or seven lines, not quite accurate, of unemotional minion type told this tale of heroism in the "Reports, Disasters, etc." column, and that was the end of it. At home, the rescued men were welcomed as if risen from the dead.

The conduct of the Coalfleets was brought to the notice of the Governor General, and in due time Hiram was presented with a gold watch and Abel with a pair of binoculars suitably inscribed.

The watch must have been lost, with other possessions, when the ironically christened *Happy Home* was wrecked on the Trinity ledges on January 3, 1881. When she fell over and sank, all hands got into the mizzen rigging. His wife and nine-year-old daughter Mary died beside Captain Coalfleet that winter night, and his legs were frozen to the knees.

Of the forgotten heroine of the *Industry,* Angeline Publicover, it is recorded that she never bought her wedding dress. In *Aes Triplex* Stevenson asks, "What woman could be lured into marriage, so much more dangerous than the wildest sea?" Angeline had had her experience of the wildest sea. She was a good girl and a brave girl. Long-drawn suffering and deadly peril only revealed the native strength of a character which must be called heroic.

Stern decoration from the barque Saladin, *now held at the Maritime Museum of the Atlantic, Halifax, Nova Scotia*

THE *SALADIN* PIRATES

To the left of the hospital drive at Halifax there is a low, round knoll encircled by a straggling fringe of young trees. I can never pass it without thinking of the story which ended there on July 30, 1844. It is a black story of sordid crime, of blood and treasure, of punishment overtaking sin. Only he who told of the homicide on board of the *Flying Scud* and the killings on Treasure Island could do it justice, but Tusitala sleeps on the top of Vaea Mountain, and the chance auditor must do what he can lest the tale be lost.

In October, 1842 Captain George Fielding sailed from Liverpool in the barque *Vitula,* a fine vessel of four hundred sixty tons, for Buenos Aires. He was son of a soldier of the 30th Regiment and had lived in Gaspé. In person he was stout, well built, with strongly marked features, by no means unpleasing. His expression denoted great decision of character, a trait essential in the master of a ship. Although not an educated man, he had picked up enough French, Spanish, Portuguese, and Dutch to make himself understood in those languages among seafaring folk. With him he took his son, George, a smart boy about fourteen years of age. Though he had been married twice and his second wife was alive, he tried to persuade a girl in a Liverpool hotel to go off with him. Before he sailed, some agent of the Naval and Military Bible Society gave him a copy of the Holy Scriptures, suitably inscribed on the title page. It was little read, being reserved for another purpose.

Finding freights low at Buenos Aires, Fielding sailed for Valparaiso. There the situation was no better, and he determined on a step which cost him his vessel. He sailed up the coast to the island of Chincha in order to smuggle a shipload of guano, the property of the Peruvian government. The authorities got wind of this bold evasion of the law and sent a force of fifty soldiers to seize the *Vitula*. Fielding, undismayed, prepared to resist them; he had firearms laid out on the deck and was in the act of cutting the cable with a carving knife, when the boatload of Peruvians came alongside. His crew of fourteen, whom he bullied and starved, ran below, but Fielding and his mate fought. Fielding was shot in the shoulder and was overpowered and brought with the *Vitula* to the port of Pisco, fourteen miles away. All the city came out to see him. He was so weak from the loss of blood, which saturated his clothing and even his shoes, that he could not walk or stand. He was set on a mule and, with two men supporting him, was sent to the convent hospital to have his wounds dressed. From Pisco he was taken to Callao, and the *Vitula* was anchored under the guns of the fort. At first he was allowed the liberty of the port, although the crew were thrown into prison. Fielding, the resourceful, hatched a scheme for cutting out his vessel at midnight and sounded various persons in the port on their willingness to help him. They informed on him, and he was put in prison. But with the help of his clever son, young George, he managed to escape in a poncho, passed the sentinel, and after hiding in the shavings and carpenter's litter of a dockyard for two days and two nights, found refuge on board a British steamer and so reached Valparaiso once more.

He was, however, a ruined man. He had lost his vessel. The Peruvian courts had condemned and sold her for fifteen thousand dollars. How was he to face the owners, Myers & Company, Liverpool, whose vessel he had flung away? Who would ever employ him again? All he had managed to save from the wreck were some clothes, charts, and instruments, and also the ship's

Bible. His son was not in custody and came to Valparaiso with him. All this happened in the month of July, 1843.

For some time Fielding remained in Valparaiso, trying to obtain a passage home. The *Jeremiah Carnett* and the *Belfast* would not take him, but Captain "Sandy" Mackenzie, of the barque *Saladin,* of Newcastle, in an evil hour for himself, agreed to give Fielding and young George a free passage to London. The *Saladin* was a beautiful barque of about five hundred fifty tons register, with a bronze figurehead of a turbaned Turk, in accordance with her name; her cabin was magnificent, with staterooms suitable for lady passengers, fitted with mahogany and other valuable woods. She was loaded with guano and about twenty tons of copper. In her run, she carried thirteen bars of silver, each weighing one hundred fifty pounds, a chestful of dollars, and a number of money letters. The master was an old-fashioned, driving, swearing, drinking, capable son of Neptune. He had followed the sea for twenty years, had acquired a competence, and was now able to retire and live ashore. He had decided that this was to be his last voyage. His plan was to settle down at Newcastle with his family. On February 8, 1844, the *Saladin* sailed from Valparaiso on what was to prove her last voyage. Including the two passengers, there were fourteen souls on board.

Apparently Mackenzie and Fielding were too much alike to get on well together. Two of a trade cannot agree, says the proverb. Before long, there were frequent quarrels between the two captains, with no assigned reason. On shipboard character manifests itself with surprising distinctness and rapidity. In a very short time, fellow passengers learn to like or dislike one another. The fact is notorious. These men soon came to hate each other and quarrelled continually, even in the hearing of the crew. Fielding sometimes refused to come to the table for his meals, and Mackenzie would tell his mate, Bryerly, that it served him right for giving him a passage. Fielding was a desperate man, ruined, with no future, and apparently from mingled motives of hatred and greed, formed a plot to get possession of the *Saladin*.

He first approached the sailmaker, George Jones, who came from County Clare. He was a man of middle size, with dark hair, full blue eyes, and heavy lowering brows. He was a cripple, having lost his leg by the fall of a spar, and like John Silver, he wore a stump. Until the Horn was rounded, Jones acted as steward and was a witness of the endless quarrels between the captains in the splendid cabin. After rounding the Horn, a young Scotsman named Galloway took his place, a fresh-coloured boy of nineteen with grey eyes and a prominent forehead. He was the son of a bookseller and he could read and write well; he even understood something of navigation. Jones went back to his sedentary sailmaking, and Fielding, after his quarrels, would come and go all over them again with Jones. He would talk to the ignorant foremast hand about the amount of money on board, what a fine prize the *Saladin* would make, and asked if he would fight if attacked by pirates, for such water-thieves were among the perils of ocean navigation as late as the forties. So he won Jones over and then used him as a tool to gain the remainder of the mate's watch.

Another of the conspirators was William Trevaskiss, who had shipped under the name of Johnson. He was a short, broad-shouldered, thick-set man, with dark blue eyes, and in them a bold, determined, forbidding expression. According to his own account, he had been discharged from the USS *Constellation* in Valparaiso, but he was more probably a deserter. To his shipmates he was "Bill," or "the red-haired man." The fourth conspirator was John Hazelton, five feet, six or seven inches in height, who claimed the north of Ireland as the place of his nativity. He was a black-haired man with neatly trimmed whiskers and large, full, bright eyes. According to one observer, he was "the beau-ideal of a pirate," which implies a standard of comparison. The fifth to join the murder pact was Charles Gustavus Anderson, a Swede from Udavalla, where his father was a master shipbuilder. He was about Hazelton's height, dark-haired, brown-eyed, and he spoke broken English. He was a mere lad, only nineteen, but he entered into the plot eagerly. When Jones broached it to him and said that "Sandy" was to be killed, the Swede cried, "By G—d, I'll take a knife and cut his throat. He shall no more strike me away from the helm." All Fielding's tools were young. The oldest was only twenty-three.

Murder was brewing on the fated *Saladin,* but none except the conspirators had the least inkling of what was coming. The secret was well kept. Once peg leg Jones attempted to give the captain a hint, but "Sandy" repulsed him with:

"You d—d Irishman, I want to hear nothing."

After getting all one watch on his side, Fielding played on their fears. Each man must now help himself through or his own life would pay the forfeit. The leader's plan was well considered, to the last detail. It was to kill the captain and mate first, then the members of the other watch as well as the cook and the steward; after gaining possession of the ship, they would sail her to some lonely harbour in Gaspé or Newfoundland, go back to the United States, return in a small vessel and carry off the dollars to spend in some foreign land. What was at the back of Fielding's brain can never be known, but from what he tried to do, it is doubtful if he ever intended that any of these ignorant tarpaulins should share in his gains.

The *Saladin* was two degrees north of the Line, in the region of calms and light baffling winds, by Friday, April 13, and the plot was ripe. All but the sailmaker were on deck; as he was not there, the attempt was postponed. Jones tried to excuse himself for hanging back, but Fielding told him:

"There is no use making a fool of yourself. If you go back, your life is no more."

On Saturday, Fielding and Mackenzie had a violent quarrel about the gig, which was heard by all the men on deck. Then Fielding told his accomplices,

"It must be done this night."

That night, or rather, early Sunday morning, it was done. The mate, Bryerly, had the middle watch from midnight till four o'clock, and with him came on deck the four men engaged to kill him. He gave Hazelton the wheel, saying:

"Jack, steer the ship as well as you can. I do not feel very well."

In the light airs anyone could steer. He went forward in his oilskin coat and lay down on the hencoop. He had made his last entry in the log the day before at noon. Once he rose from the hencoop and asked Captain Fielding to go below. Fielding said he would, but first he went forward and spoke to the watch. Bryerly lay down on the coop again for his last sick slumber. The day before, the carpenter had been working on deck, and his tools, claw-hammer, broadaxe, maul, adze, and the rest lay in the stern of the longboat. The four, Fielding, Trevaskiss, Jones, and Anderson crept aft silently, armed themselves from the carpenter's tools, and gathered around the unconscious mate. Trevaskiss brought down his axe; the unfortunate man had only time for a single cry, and Fielding, Trevaskiss, and Anderson bundled the body overside. Then Fielding came to Hazelton at the wheel:

"There is one gone," he whispered.

Then followed an anxious, quavering time in the dark. The murderers were undecided what to do next. There were four of them, armed with lethal weapons, but they feared to attack Mackenzie single in his berth. They peered through the skylight into the after-cabin to see if he was asleep. At last the Swede and black-whiskered Hazelton stole down the companionway. There was a long silence. Jones, the shaking coward at the wheel, let the ship run up into the wind repeatedly in his agitation, and Fielding would take it out of his hands and put her back on her course. Then the two crept up the companionway again. They had done nothing. "Sandy's" brown dog watched beside his master. He growled or stirred at their approach, and they were afraid he would bite them. In the silence of the tropical night the captain's bell rang twice, but no one attended to it. The *Saladin* made her quiet way through the broad waters.

They then decided to kill the carpenter, who lived in the steerage. Fielding stationed Trevaskiss, Hazelton, and the Swede around the hatch and called their victim up into the ambush. Before he reached the deck, Anderson struck him heavily with his own hammer. He fell forward stunned, or at least not killed outright. The three dragged him up and flung him over the side, but the water revived him and he made some outcry as he went astern. This gave Fielding the opportunity he wanted. Ambushing his murderers around the companionway, he raised the cry of "Man overboard!" At the same time, Jones rattled the skylight and joined in the cry. It brought the captain flying up the companionway in his shirt, shouting to the steersman:

"Put the helm hard down!"

As his head came above the companionway, Anderson, who was standing on the scuttle, struck him, but the blow injured him little. Mackenzie sprang at his assailant. Anderson ran to the break of the poop, then turned and grappled with his captain. Fielding shouted to Jones:

"D—n you, why don't you run after him? If you don't lay hold of him, I'll give you a clout that will kill you."

Jones left the wheel and flung his arms around Mackenzie's neck. The luckless man had time to realize his plight and recognize his murderer. He cried, "Oh, Captain Fielding—" when his charity passenger struck him twice with his broadaxe, saying:

"Oh, d—n you, I'll give it to you."

Mackenzie fell to the deck. Fielding hauled the body forward of the companionway and struck it again, and then flung it overboard. His son, young George, stood by shouting, "Give it to him."

Three men killed! It was nerve-racking work, and more was to be done. Fielding, Hazelton, Anderson, and Trevaskiss went into the cabin to get a drink. Then the wooden-legged man was relieved at the wheel and he, too, went below for a supply of Dutch courage. When Fielding came on deck again, he said to his son:

"I am captain."

Young George had regrets. He replied:

"It was a pity I had not a blow at Sandy."

For some time the murderers stood on the quarterdeck consulting what to do next. There were still four lives to take. In order to arouse no suspicions, Fielding was to conceal himself in the companionway. Young George was behind him at the foot of the ladder, armed with a carving knife, under his father's orders to "stick" the first man who should come down. Jones was to lie down in the longboat, Anderson was to lean against the mainmast pretending to be asleep, while Hazelton and Trevaskiss should go to call the morning watch. The plan succeeded to admiration.

There was a pretence of hauling down the flying-jib and the captain's watch was called. It was Jem Allen's trick at the wheel. When the sleepy man came aft to relieve Hazelton, he paused for a moment and stood facing the stern, for a reason all sailors will understand. Nothing was further from his thoughts than death when Anderson stole up behind and struck him in the back of the head with an axe. The force of the blow sent the man overboard, Fielding watching all the while from the shadow of the companionway. Then he said to Hazelton, relieving him at the wheel:

"Jack, you have done nothing yet. Take that axe!"

The order, as Hazelton stated afterwards, was "strict," and, as he was afraid of being killed, he obeyed. Thomas Moffat came sleepily and unsuspiciously on deck and sat down on a spar near the galley, with his two good shipmates, Hazelton and Travaskiss, on each side of him. As Moffat turned his head toward the bow,

Trevaskiss nodded to Hazelton to strike. He struck with the axe, and Trevaskiss struck, and Moffat fell to the deck bleeding like a stuck pig. A third seaman, Samuel Collins, had gone into the head as lookout. After felling Moffat, Hazelton sang out to Anderson to "finish" Collins. One blow in the skull finished him, and he sank through the rigging to the sea.

Six men murdered within an hour or so! In all the seven seas that peaceful Sunday morning was there a stranger ship afloat than the elegant *Saladin,* rocking in the doldrums! Again and again her deck had been the scene of murder most foul, and through it all two men had slept the heavy sleep of tired sailors. These were the cabin boy, Galloway, and William Carr, the cook, a stocky, pock-marked, fresh-coloured Englishman from North Shields, who could read and write and carried a well-worn pocket Bible. They also were marked for death and Fielding, the resolute, was all for having them go the way of the others, but his butchers were sick of their bloody work and would not consent to their shipmates' death. Perhaps it was the daylight, which showed them what they had done.

About six o'clock, Carr awoke and turned out to his duty as usual. Like Bryerly, he had been sick for a couple of days. As he came aft to the galley, he saw on the starboard side by the foremast backstay a great quantity of blood, where poor Moffat had been felled like an ox. On the poop stood Fielding and his four accomplices. The helmsman had called them up from the cabin when he saw Carr on deck. The cook was slow to realize what had happened and came farther aft to inquire the reason for the blood, when Fielding bade him halt.

"What is the matter?" Carr asked in confusion.

"Come up. We will not harm you." Carr came up the ladder crying like a child with fear, and asked again: "What is the matter?"

"I am commander of this vessel now."

"What does this mean?"

"The master and crew have gone away and left us," replied Fielding. Carr glanced around the empty sea and then at the *Saladin*'s deck. All the boats were in their places.

"It is impossible," he gasped. "It can't be the case—all the boats are about the ship."

Fielding then spoke out.

"We have finished Sandy. We shall have no more cursing and swearing now. We have finished the carpenter, mate, and Jemmy, Moffat, and Sam." Carr looked down at the feet of the murderers and saw their bloody tools, recognizing a small hatchet of his own, and the carpenter's adze, maul, and hammer, and he thought he was within a hair's breadth of his death. Amid his tears and sobs, he managed to stammer:

"It is a serious circumstance."

Said Fielding: "Will you join us?"

"If I do not," said poor Carr, "I suppose I must go the same road as the rest."

The sailors sang out that he should not go overboard. Hazelton made the trembling man sit down on the skylight and tried to quiet him. No more lives were to be taken and, disappointed, Fielding told him to go down into the cabin for some grog. Young George gave him something out of a bottle, which he needed badly to steady his nerves, and then he went forward to light the galley fire and prepare breakfast. Nearly all that day he was crying for fear. Well he might. As soon as his back was turned, Fielding told his tools that when they got near land he would kill these two and the "Dutchman." Galloway, the cabin boy, had followed Carr on deck laughing, and, when he learned of the murders, wished that he could have had a "cut at Sandy." He agreed to share the lot of the pirates.

The ship was put about, and Fielding shaped the course northwest and by north, away from London and towards Newfoundland. The remnant of the crew were divided into watches, Carr, Galloway, and Hazelton forming one. After breakfast, Fielding spent the morning rummaging the papers, letter bags, and desks in the after-cabin. A number of money letters were burnt by his orders after the money enclosed had been taken from them. He locked the spirits from the men, and it was observed that he drank heavily himself. Even his iron nerves needed artificial strength. There were some arms on board and these the crew threw overboard, except a cutlass and Captain Mackenzie's fowling-piece, which Fielding said they might need to shoot seabirds. Their butchering tools, two hatchets, the carpenter's broadaxe, adze, and large hammer also went over the side, "lest," said Captain Fielding, "we should get jealous of one another."

Being the Christian Sabbath, the day was not allowed to pass without some form of religious observance. Fielding called the crew into the fine, mahogany-fitted cabin, where they had spliced the main-brace that morning and boasted, as the liquor took hold, which was the best murderer. He explained that it was best for all to swear "to be brotherly together," and he brought out his Bible, which had shared his adventures from Liverpool around the Horn and back again thus far, and which he had preserved when he lost the *Vitula*. In turn, each blood-guilty man kissed the book and swore to be "loyal and brotherly" to the rest. So did Fielding, who was even then plotting the murder of the men he was swearing to fidelity. His son was not required to take the oath, being too young.

One thinks of the homicides on the deck of the *Flying Scud*, repeating the Lord's Prayer in unison.

The murder plot had been a complete success. The ship with all its wealth was in the hands of Fielding and his assassins, but a black atmosphere of suspicion descended at once upon that fatal and perfidious barque. That same night, Trevaskiss told Carr and Galloway that Fielding meant to do for them and that if they went he would lose his life as well. So these three formed some sort of pact, an offensive-defensive alliance. When Trevaskiss went below at eight o'clock, the end of his watch, he found that, by the captain's orders, Carr and Galloway were to berth forward in the forecastle, while all the rest were to live in the cabin. He asked his mates why the cook and the cabin boy were not allowed the same privileges. He was referred to the new captain, and Fielding answered:

"We can't trust them."

"If you are afraid, I am not," said Trevaskiss, "and if they sleep in the forecastle, so will I."

He carried his point. All shared the same quarters. Fielding's scheme to divide the men and finish them in detail was thwarted. He had foolishly told Trevaskiss that he would poison Carr and Galloway when they got near land. He also approached Galloway and Anderson separately to help to get rid of the others.

On Monday there was a division of Mackenzie's clothes and effects. Carr and Fielding had a difference over a pair of new trousers, which the captain wanted for his son. In the afternoon, they set the fore topmast stunsail. At six, all hands had tea in the cabin, after which Carr set some bread in the galley, returned to the cabin, and lay down in one of the beds until he should be called to take his turn at the wheel at eight. While there, Fielding came down, took the cabin light into the pantry, and muffled it with the tablecloth. Then he went into the after-cabin. What he was doing there Carr could not make out, but from the sounds, it seemed that he was loading the fowling-piece. He was capable of any treachery. The Bible oath and Fielding's cure for "jealousy" did not prove completely efficacious.

When Carr went on deck, the rest of the hands came down into the cabin. Then ensued a turbulent, confused, wrangling scene that lasted for hours. Under the cabin-table, Trevaskiss had previously discovered two horse-pistols. Everybody thought that all the arms had been thrown overboard except the fowling-piece. Now Hazelton drew the pistols out of their hiding place and said:

"These mean something. Who put them there?"

Everyone denied all knowledge of them.

There was a further search for weapons. In the locker, a large copper canister full of powder was discovered, and in the spirit-locker, of which Fielding had the key, the carving knife which had been missing since Sunday. In the locker were also two bottles of brandy, which from the taste the sailors thought were poisoned. All these were taken on deck with the fowling-piece and thrown over the side. Fielding denied all knowledge of the knife and tried to turn the men from their purpose by the offer of grog, but they now realized that it was their life or his, and they were not to be denied. Fielding threatened and stormed. He told them, what was the truth, that they were all afraid of him, and at last, he tried to regain the deck. He said he would throw himself overboard and turned to the door. Then they fell on him and bound him hand and foot, he screaming, shouting, daring them to kill him. At last they gagged him, and in that condition he passed the night in the cabin under constant guard, while the hands consulted how to dispose of him. Hazelton was for confining him in the forecastle and putting him ashore the first land they made. Carr said he could never sleep while Fielding lived. But the four others declared they would not lend a hand to another man's death as long as they were in the ship. It was a long wrangle in the cabin of that fated vessel, while Fielding, gagged and tied hand and foot, sat helpless and heard it all. In those long hours he must have savoured all the bitterness of death.

That night no one slept in the *Saladin*. Fear reigned. The sailors dreaded that their tyrant might get free. They kept the boy from his father lest he should help him. So the watches passed till the dawn of Tuesday, April 17. The morning brought counsel.

About seven, Fielding's feet were unbound and he was brought on deck. By this time the liquor must have died out of him; he must have understood that his last hour had come. Even now, he was not at the end of his resources. He begged Galloway, who was at the wheel, to cast him loose and he would save his life a second time.

Then the four most deeply dyed in blood, Jones, Hazelton, Anderson, and Trevaskiss, decided that Carr and Galloway, the two who had as yet "done nothing," must share their guilt by killing Fielding. Galloway refused, but the others compelled him to touch their baffled leader. Carr and Jones carried him aft and heaved him into the sea.

It takes about four minutes to drown....

Then Carr and Galloway seized young George and put him overside, at the larboard gangway. He screamed and tore their clothes and clung to them. They shook him off....

The others sat about the deck and watched both scenes.

After this they got at the liquor, and every day some of the crew were drunk. They made Galloway navigator as he had the most education, and he kept the reckoning in a memorandum book. But as the old ballad of the *Saladin* runs:

> We mostly kept before the wind,
> For we could do no more.

They lived at rack and manger in the cabin. They threw some of the copper overboard to lighten the ship and some they used to sink the gig. They nailed a board over the name on the stern, and they painted the bronze Turk at the bow white, clumsy expedients to conceal the identity of the vessel. They planned to scuttle her and escape with the dollars in the one remaining boat, but they waited just a little too long.

On the morning of May 22, 1844, the *Saladin*, with all sails set, even to her royals, drove hard on the island at the mouth of Country Harbour, Nova Scotia, at a place ever since called Saladin Point.

On hearing that a large vessel was ashore, Captain Cunningham of the schooner *Billow* manned his boat and went to her assistance. He found everything in the greatest confusion onboard, the disorder in the cabin being especially offensive to his sailorly eye. He stood by for thirty-six hours putting things to rights. The sailors, honest fellows, had a plausible story about their captain dying at sea and the mate and several hands being washed off the yard. Since then, they had lived rather freely. But their stories did not agree very well. There were instruments belonging to a Captain Fielding, who they said had died at Valparaiso. The last entry in the log was for April 14. Suspicion grew, and in the end, the six honest sailormen were arrested and brought to Halifax in HMS *Fair Rosamond*. The poor, mishandled *Saladin* became a total wreck, but the value of the silver, copper, and cash salvaged from her and deposited in the Bank of Nova Scotia was 18,000 pounds sterling. Perhaps it was as well that the *Saladin* went to pieces, for none would ever want to sail in that death-ship again.

There was a legal difficulty to overcome. Crime had plainly been committed, but it had been committed on the high seas outside the jurisdiction of any Nova Scotian court. So a special court was constituted in which the admiral of the station sat as judge in all the splendour of full naval uniform beside the chief justice, and three puisne judges. Legal formalities were hardly needed for, while in their cells in the old penitentiary on the Northwest Arm, Carr and Galloway sent for a lawyer and made a clean breast of their share in the murders. They likewise confessed the crimes of their shipmates, which they did not witness, as they were below and asleep at the time. Carr's statement is clear, coherent, and brief, showing decided intelligence. No doubt all hands had discussed the sequence of events and the various details many times. The confessions of Jones, Trevaskiss, Hazelton, and Anderson followed, almost as a matter of course.

To find them guilty and sentence them to death was the only course open to the court. The plea was changed from piracy, which involved hanging in chains, to plain murder, and they were sentenced all four to be hanged by the neck until they were dead. Carr and Galloway were also tried for the murder of the two Fieldings, but the plea was made that they were forced to do the deed by their shipmates, and so they were acquitted.

The execution was a public spectacle long remembered in Halifax. The South Common was bare of buildings then, except for the little chapel "built in a day" standing in the Catholic cemetery. On the small eminence opposite, the scaffold was erected. At each end of the platform was an upright post, and a stout beam, from which dangled four nooses, joined them. The four "drops" were held in place by simple wooden buttons, controlled by a single cord. One pull of the cord opened the four trap doors simultaneously.

Early on July 30, 1844, a company of the 52nd Foot formed a circle around the scaffold and kept the spectators at a proper distance. All the city turned out to see the sight. About ten o'clock a procession came along Tower Road; first the sheriff in a gig, then the four murderers in two closed carriages. Three Catholic priests attended the two Irishmen, and an Anglican clergyman, Trevaskiss and the Swede. On each side marched a strong body of the First Royals with fixed bayonets. The four condemned men mounted the platform and took their places on the four trap doors. They took farewell of one another and shook hands. Jones kissed his fellows on the cheek and said a few words to the crowd to the effect that he was an Irishman from Clare, that he was sorry for what he had done, and that he hoped for pardon from God. Imprisonment had taken the sailors' tan from their cheeks; they looked debilitated, but placid. Anderson alone seemed unconcerned and looked over the heads of the crowd to the blue, sparkling sea. Hazelton and Jones handed their written confessions to their spiritual advisors. The priests knelt in prayer, the control cord was pulled, and the four men dropped to their death. In three-quarters of an hour the bodies were cut down. Hazelton and Jones were buried in the Catholic cemetery, but Trevaskiss and Anderson were inearthed in the paupers' burying ground. Anderson was dug up and anatomised by a certain young doctor, and his skull may be seen to this day in the Provincial Museum.

This is the tragedy of the *Saladin.* Of the fourteen persons who sailed in her from Valparaiso on February 8, 1844, only two remained alive on July 30. In all the annals of the sea, there is scarce a record of more revolting crime.

Of these two survivors, Galloway disappeared, but Carr, according to local tradition, settled down in Digby county and died there not very long ago. He had noted peculiarities. For one thing he rarely walked, but always went at a "shepherd's trot." He was a very respectable man, a pillar of a local church, but once a year on the anniversary of his crime he drowned remembrance in liquor.

Ballads were made on the affair which still cling to the memory of Nova Scotians. The blood-stained hatch was long preserved in the museum, but has recently disappeared. The *Saladin*'s cabin windows were built into a carpenter's shop in Country Harbour, and some people believe that pirate treasure may yet be found where the fatal vessel went ashore.

The Research *in a storm. Painting by an unknown artist.*

THE SAGA OF "RUDDER" CHURCHILL

In the great days of sail, all the counties of Nova Scotia built wooden ships, but Yarmouth, county and shiretown, stood apart in a class by themselves. Hants might run neck and neck in tonnage and using Georgia pine build admittedly better ships; it might plume itself on constructing the *W. D. Lawrence,* the biggest ship ever built in Nova Scotia; there might be seventeen captains of clan MacKenzie at one time sailing out of Pictou; but nothing ever shook the primacy of Yarmouth as the most maritime county of a maritime province. Between this county and all the others, there was a cleavage. Thirty-five Nova Scotia vessels might be lying together in Antwerp docks, but the Yarmouth skippers kept themselves to themselves. Meeting other captains from the province in the street, they could pass the time of day, but their intercourse went no further. Bright, hospitable Yarmouth town is built on shipping, and *Ab Urbe Condita,* Yarmouth families have followed the sea. From generation to generation, Lovitts, Canns, and Killams, Hatfields, Cooks, and Churchills have commanded ships with varying fortunes in every ocean. The historical shallop *Pompey* of twenty-five tons, which brought the first settlers to the county in 1761, became the fruitful mother of whole fleets of every rig and every size, until Yarmouth could boast the largest *per capita* tonnage of any port in the world.

Perhaps the reason for Yarmouth's pride in her ships and sailormen and why her master mariners were inclined to bear themselves with a difference may appear from this true tale of the ship *Research* and her commander, "Rudder" Churchill.

The *Research* was a large, full-rigged ship of 1,459 tons burden, built in Yarmouth in 1861 by Thomas Killam, a well-known merchant of that town. On November 10, 1866, she sailed from Quebec deeply laden with ton-timber consigned to William Lindsay & Co. of Glasgow. Those were the days of rafts. Huge, picturesque, floating islands of wood with sails and oars, with shanties on them and fires burning were water-borne down the St. Lawrence to Quebec. Here they were broken up, and the square "sticks," fifty or sixty feet long, were loaded through the bow-ports of the timber droghers for the United Kingdom. The coves of Quebec were full of these vessels, three hundred at a time, painted frigate fashion with black, dummy ports on a broad white streak. The *Research* was in this trade. Besides the timber in her hold, she carried a deckload of deals, packed and leashed and wedged together into an immoveable mass. It was very late in the season for such a voyage.

Her captain was George Churchill of Yarmouth, aged twenty-nine. His photograph shows a bearded, gentle, almost dreamy face, but there was nothing vague about his seamanship, and his resolution was iron. He was known as "Tear" Churchill, but how he acquired the violent by-name is not clear. He was a navigator of much experience, well reputed for having extricated his ship from dangerous situations and for once having saved it from destruction by fire. The first mate was his nephew, Aaron Flint Churchill, a young giant of sixteen with more than his share of the family's good looks. He had already been two years at sea, and he was second in command by virtue of his ability, and not by any board of trade certificate.

Flint is a Yarmouth family name, but it betokens the quality of his will. If he had never done so before, he was to prove his manhood in this voyage. George Marshall, also a Yarmouth man, was boatswain, and every inch a sailor. As always, the officers were the spearhead of the less resolute crew.

More than a fortnight was spent in getting down the river, but, by the night of November 26, the *Research* was clear of the dangerous Straits of Belle Isle and fairly out on the Atlantic. That night the wind almost died away and the barometer fell to 28°, a most ominous hint of trouble to come. Every precaution was taken. Sail was reduced at once to close-reefed topsails. The *Research* carried double topsails, Forbes's patent, which means that the second sail from the deck on each mast was in two parts, with two yards. Close-reefing meant only the lower half showing. The yards were braced around inboard to present the least resistance to the wind. With all made snug, as the sailors say, the *Research*, stripped like an athlete, awaited the onslaught of the storm. All night the uncanny lull continued, but with the morning the tempest broke. Out of the northwest it came, a typical winter storm from the frozen Pole, with a fury and a violence which Elizabethan seamen would term outrageous. It smote the *Research* like the hammer of Thor. It ripped the three topsails from the yards and flung them on the waves, leaving only streamers of canvas whipping from the bolt-ropes. Worse was to follow. A tremendous sea struck the rudder and broke the rudder-stock a little below the casing, or opening in the stem through which the stock passes, to connect with the tiller and the wheel. The same deadly blow snapped the half-inch links of the rudder-chains. The latter led from a large ring-bolt on the back of the rudder to the rail, or the quarter. They might be called emergency or safety chains, because if the stock were broken, the ship could still be steered by means of tackles shackled onto them. Now both stock and chains were broken. The vessel was definitely out of control. The gale, which began with such force, continued, with one brief lull, for a whole month, growing ever worse and worse.

Short of total dismasting, the plight of the *Research* could hardly be more desperate. She could carry no sail, her rudder was useless, and worse than useless, for it was pounding heavily against the rudder-post. The rudder-post is not, as its name might imply, a single piece of wood, but a complex of strong timbers heavily backed by other timbers framed together with all the shipwright's art. It holds the afterpart of a vessel together, as the keystone holds the arch. Injury to it may mean a fatal leak. Without a sail, without a rudder, the *Research* drove helplessly before the winter storm. A rudderless ship in a storm is a proverb for impotence and disaster.

The rudder is the most important part of a ship. St. James, with his experience of navigation on Galilee, was impressed with the contrast between the great ship and the small rudder which yet turned the ship about withersoever the governor listed. But if the rudder is hopelessly disabled like the rudder of the *Research,* what then? Something must be done, and George Churchill was not the man to fold his hands and resign himself to calamity. Attempts were made to pass a hawser over the stern, around the wildly flinging rudder, and so hobble it. The expedient served only for a short time. The hawser chafed through, and the pounding rudder began to break up. How to fetter the massive piece of mechanism and prevent further damage was the problem. If tackles could be affixed to the big ring-bolt on the back of the rudder, it could be controlled and the ship steered from the deck. But the rudder of a loaded vessel is practically all under water, and the *Research* was wallowing in mountainous seas. The first thing to do was to lighten the ship aft and so bring the ring-bolt to the surface. The careful stowage of the deckload had to be undone and the bright, fresh-cut deals thrown overboard. It was a long and dangerous job, but it was done. The *Research* was down by the head, with the stern considerably higher than the bow. And all the time, the gale blew harder, and the billows swept the deck, and the spray froze where it fell.

The next morning was November 28. The stern of the *Research* was now sufficiently elevated to permit of tackles being fastened to the ring-bolt on the back of the rudder. There was but one way to fasten them: a man must go down into the water and affix them. As the stern projected far over the rudder, as the rudder itself was constantly battered to and fro by the fierce waves, the difficulties of such a task must be plain to the meanest capacity. And who was to do the job? It is in such emergencies that the first mate comes to the fore. On that bitter winter morning, Aaron Churchill stripped to the buff and went over the side in a bowline.

"He wouldn't be much colder without his clothes," said the port warden reflectively when he heard of the incident.

Going over the side in a bowline, even in bad weather, is no uncommon feat for a sailor. When the staunch but mishandled *Osberga* began to leak through her bow-ports, which should never have been cut in her, Captain David Douglas went down in a bowline to repair the damage. He was often six feet under water. Charles Doty, first mate of the *Native,* was four hours in the water passing a chain lashing around her rudder which had come adrift, but he spent three months in a New York hospital afterwards. Captain Borden Marsh did the same thing during his fortnight of starvation on board the brigantine *Cleo.* The port warden himself learned what the pressure of the water can be, as he dangled in a bowline. But the circumstances attending Aaron Churchill's feat are, one may say, unique.

Bowline is a sea term with several meanings. It is, in the first place, the safest knot a sailor makes. It is simple, quickly tied, and it will not slip. Bowline also means a rope with a loop in it fastened with this safe knot. The sailor sits in this loop, and thus can be swayed up to the masthead, if necessary. As the port warden demonstrated with the domestic clothesline, what Aaron Churchill sat in was a double bowline. One loop went round the thighs; the second went under one armpit and over the opposite shoulder. Each loop draws against the other, and the knot is just over the heart, thus leaving both hands free. In such a harness of three-inch rope was the first mate of the *Research* lowered over the side and into water with a temperature somewhere near the freezing point. With one hand he held the tackle, a hooked block or pulley through which ropes ran. The hook must be slipped through the ring, when opportunity offered. This was a one hand job. Churchill needed his other hand to save himself from being battered to death against the side, or the overhang, of the vessel. On the deck above him, men paid out the line or stood by to haul and watched and lifted when the waves swept over the man below. It is safe to infer that the master and the boatswain managed the rope on which hung the fate of the ship.

"Impossible!" said the port warden, in the voice he used to hail the masthead with, when he came to this part of the story. "He may have gone over in a bowline, but never in that weather. Why, he would have been smashed up against the counter and killed. He might have gone down perpendicular, but never under the stem."

The port warden was very decided and emphatic. But the evidence is irrefragable. Here are the contemporary accounts in *The Times* and *The Glasgow Daily Herald;* here are the entries in Captain Churchill's own handwriting preserved by his niece Margery in Yarmouth. Family tradition has handed down precise detail which could not have been invented. Years afterwards, when he was a rich man, Aaron Churchill had a picture painted. It represents a full-rigged ship in a violent storm and a man hanging by a line under the stern. A reproduction of it states specifically that the man in the bowline is Aaron Churchill. The fact is well attested, but the scepticism of a practical sailor like the port warden shows that this deed is unique, even in the marvellous chronicles of death-defying first mates.

That bitter November day, Aaron Churchill needed all his wonderful strength and vitality. In years a boy, he was already a man grown, half an inch over six feet, perfectly proportioned, with muscles of iron. Freezing water, icy wind, drowning, broken bones, being battered to death against the overhanging counter were some of the dangers he had to face. Besides, the huge, heavy rudder was never at rest, but beating continually against the rudder-post with terrifying violence. Frozen, blinded, half-strangled, Churchill must watch for the favourable second when the ring-bolt was near enough for him to slip the hook of the tackle into it. Victor Hugo imagined a fight between a man and an inanimate object which seemed endowed with demoniac life, the gunner and the carronade adrift between decks in the *Claymore;* but under the stern of the *Research,* a mother-naked man waged a real battle against the brute force of a huge piece of mechanism, which, as it flung incalculably to and fro, threatened every instant to maim or kill him. That day Aaron Churchill was fighting not for his own life, but for the lives of all on board. Impossible as it seems, it is yet a fact that he did what he went down to do. The Churchills have the name of being "dogged." After an hour and a half of incredible labour, he succeeded in hooking one tackle into the ring-bolt. He was hauled up on board insensible and laid out on the deck to recover. Half a pint of brandy was poured down his throat. Slowly he revived, slowly his strength returned, and then,—he went down over the side of the ship with the second tackle.

113

This time he was down for an hour and three-quarters by the clock, one hundred and five minutes of freezing, of strangulation, of desperate exertion, but somehow or other he managed to fasten the second tackle in the ring. One more typical first mate's job was done. The dangerous rudder was securely hobbled; the *Research* was once more under control and could be steered by the ancient device of pulling and hauling on the tackles. Aaron Churchill was dragged back to the deck more dead than alive, or as the unemotional *Times* report has it, "when taken on board was insensible, but recovered."

With the help of the sails the vessel was kept on her course until the 29th, that is until the next day. By the will of the master and not by the will of the storm, the bowsprit of the *Research* pointed eastward to Greenock, her port of destination. But wind and wave are pitiless antagonists. The results so painfully obtained by Aaron Churchill at the risk of his life hardly lasted twenty-four hours. On the 29th what was left of the rudder was torn from the pintles and swept away. Even a damaged rudder was better than none, and now the *Research* had not even a fragment of hers left.

Such accidents were not uncommon in the old days of sail. Captain Samuels of the flash packet *Dreadnaught* of the Black Ball Line lost his rudder off the Banks of Newfoundland. He took in his head-sails, backed his yards, and navigated his famous vessel six hundred miles, stern first, to the Azores. With a broken rudder-stock, two days out of Philadelphia, Farquhar of the *Cumberland* got tackles on his rudder and steering "pulley-haul" brought his ship across the Atlantic. The resourceful sailor had other expedients in such emergencies. He could tow a cask or a spar astern, or he could even construct a rudder. Archie Campbell of the *Piscataqua* and his mate Joe Blois built and shipped a jury-rudder when the original was lost. They saved ship and cargo, and the underwriters of Havre gave the captain a gold watch. In the examinations of their certificates, would-be mates and masters were often asked how to rig a jury-rudder. It was naturally considered a most important point.

A rudder must be strong. As built in the shipyard, its nucleus or core was the stock, a single timber of seasoned white oak, long enough to reach from the keel up through the opening in the deck, the whole depth of the vessel. To this central timber were firmly bolted a massive forepiece and a backpiece, so fashioned that the three were as if hewn out of the trunk of a single tree. It was attached to the stern-post by three right-angled hooks or pintles fitting into corresponding "gudgeons" or rings. Though so huge and massive, a rudder had to be built scientifically, so that a line drawn through the three pintles would run through the axis of the stock. To build such a rudder on board and hang it in a winter gale so that the stock would come through the casing and the pintles drop accurately into the gudgeons was manifestly impossible. Rigging a jury-rudder was a different matter.

A jury-rudder was often made in two pieces, consisting of the stock and the rudder itself. The latter was simply an oblong mass of heavy planking bolted together lengthwise and crosswise, as firm as the ship carpenter's art could make it. No attempt was made to give it the correct, original, oar-like shape. This rude substitute was hinged to the stock by stout rope lashings, or better still, by chain grummets running around the stock and through auger-holes in the top and bottom of the rudder. The whole, heavy, clumsy contrivance with all its trailing ropes attached had to be hoisted outboard, lowered over the stern, and the stock drawn up through the casing. Through the top and bottom of the rudder ran stout ropes or chains, if available, for they do not stretch, which were carried far forward on each side of the ship and hauled taut. These would draw the rudder hard against the rudder-stock and hold both firmly against the rudder-post. To make the mechanics of the device plain to the landsman's comprehension, it might be said that this homemade rudder was tied to the stern by four strings. By means of two other strings attached to the outer edge of the rudder by a looped rope called a bridle and also carried far forward, the rudder was pulled this way or that at the word of command.

To construct even such a rudder involved much hard labour with edge-tools, adjusting, calculating, measuring, shaping, sawing, hammering, boring, joining, on the reeling deck of the labouring *Research*. Aaron Churchill gets the credit of having done most of the actual work. The deckload of deals was not all started overboard; enough remained to supply materials for more than one or two jury-rudders. For two days and two nights, the big timber-ship drove impotently before the storm, while officers and men toiled at the indispensable steering gear or snatched a mouthful of food or an hour's sleep. On the morning of December 2, the jury-rudder was completed. It was being lowered over the stern when a wicked cross-sea caught it and snapped the hawser like a thread. Away floated the rudder. All this painful labour was useless.

This sudden failure might have daunted any but a Nova Scotian shipmaster, but George Churchill was as fertile in devices as that other sailorman of ancient song, the many-counselled Ulysses. He made a steering-oar. The wheelhouse had been wrecked by the hammering seas. Churchill tore down what remained of it in order to have a clear field for his next experiment. The *Research* carried spare spars, roughed out in four or in eight, lashed to the bulwark stanchions. Churchill took a spare topmast about sixty feet long, and to one end he bolted a huge square of the deckload deals. It must have looked like a wooden spade for Gargantua. This would be secured to the rail by strong lashings, which still would permit of its being moved to and fro. Other stout ropes would hold the inboard end in place. Like the jury-rudder, this enormous steering oar would be moved to port or starboard by means of lines fastened to the spade itself, and carried far forward. So it was made. Apparently it was ready for use the very next day, December 3, and hoisted into position. But it was a failure. It did not affect the vessel's way. She would not pay off before the wind. By lightening the *Research* aft, in order to get at the ring-bolt in the rudder, the stern was lifted high out of the water. It was therefore necessary to jettison part of the deckload forward in order to restore her trim. So it was done.

On December 4, the huge steering-oar was again hoisted over the stern, but it could not be sunk deep enough in the water to influence the way of the *Research;* she was a big ship. It had to be taken on board and weighted, perhaps with "thirteen fathoms of chain," or even an anchor. Next day, it was again hoisted out;

the necessary leverage was gained, but the weight was too much for the spar. The handle of the spade was fractured by the strain, about ten feet from the upper end. In spite of the break, these unconquerable sailormen got their vessel under control, and by the aid of their damaged rudder and also by deft management of such scanty canvas as they dared to set in that living gale, they sent the *Research* storming along eastward, and ever eastward. When they could take advantage of it, the tempest's fury was driving them towards their destination. The directing will of the master was guiding his ship to her predetermined goal.

Painfully the damaged steering-oar was hauled on board. Once more there was heavy carpenter-and-joiner work on the iced and reeling deck, where no landsman could even keep his footing. From the 6th to the 9th of December, the vessel drove ahead without steering-gear of any kind. By December 9 the oar was spliced and repaired, but in attempting to hoist it out, the ropes gave way and let the huge concern down on the deck, where it had to be secured and lashed fast. Amongst other minor jobs of this voyage was bending fresh canvas. Those three lost topsails had to be replaced. The port warden says that it is not necessary to send down the yards; sails properly rolled and stoppered, he avers, can be bent on in a gale of wind.

Nature is pitiless. The furious storm not only continued but grew more and more malignant, as if the elemental rage were bent solely on defeating these toiling pigmies and overwhelming the cockleshell in which they trusted. Moving hills of water broke over the helpless *Research,* smashing in the forward deckhouse where the crew lived and wrecking the provision locker. Soon they were on short allowance, and before the voyage ended their food ran out altogether.

No stauncher vessels ever swam than the best products of Nova Scotian shipyards, but no fabric of man's handiwork could endure for weeks such battering from wind and wave as befell the *Research* without showing the effects. She began to leak. The oakum in the two big bow-ports worked out and the sea came in. A timber-laden vessel cannot sink, but she can become water-logged, a helpless, unnavigable hulk below the level of the waves. To avoid this calamity for days and weeks, day and night, spell and spell about, officers and men laboured at the wheel-pumps amidships, two at the handles and others tailing onto the ropes. Constant pumping kept the water down but could not prevent it from coming in.

Still in spite of wet and cold and exposure and the heart-breaking labour at the pumps, the men of the *Research* built a third rudder, and during a lull on the morning of December 14, they got it "shipped," that is, tied on behind, like jury-rudder number one. For a whole day, this clumsy contrivance functioned and the vessel answered to her helm, but on the 15th, the violent seas smashed the stock, and the rudder was useless.

Evidently the stock of this latest failure was jammed in the casing or trunk and it was with no little trouble that Churchill and his men worried the massive wooden post out of the hole. For nearly another week, they could do nothing but hold on and work the pumps. All that time, the *Research* was wallowing in the trough and swept by "high, irregular seas" raised by hurricane weather. On this account, the narrative continues, apologetically, it was "impossible to begin work earlier" than December 21. To make matters worse, one pump was now disabled. But on the 21st, a new rudder, number four, was begun. When it was finished is not recorded, but by January 2, 1867, it was got into its place, "after much labour." This rudder held, but it was not powerful enough to control the way of the vessel. "It was necessary to put an additional rudder over the stern, like a steering-oar, worked with tackles from in-board." It is difficult to keep tally of Churchill's inventions, but this makes rudder number five. Navigating a leaking ship in hurricane weather with two jury-rudders, the men pulling and hauling on two sets of tackles at the word of command must have presented difficulties, but

Churchill the indomitable met them, overcame them, and kept his vessel on her course until January 5, when "the stock of the other was carried away and the rudder lost." And now rudder number four is out of the saga.

Somehow or other, about the turn of the year, the leaking, rudderless, crippled *Research* had traversed the Western Ocean from the Straits of Belle Isle to a position within fifty miles of Tory Island at the north of Ireland. Then she was about one hundred miles as the gull flies from her port of destination. And then,—the gale came around to eastward, dead in her teeth. "A series of hurricanes and heavy seas" drove her back and back, south and west, out into the Atlantic, eighteen hundred miles out of her course.

Away from the north of Ireland to the neighbourhood of the Azores, the *Research* was scourged and driven. Still more harm was done her by the hammering seas. They "swept the decks, stove in the hatches and carried away bulwarks." Let the layman who has noted the massive strength of hatches and bulwarks estimate the weight of water which would smash them down from above or tear them from the ship's solid frame. With Scottish reserve, *The Glasgow Daily Herald* remarks, "The officers and men were frequently greatly exhausted, and upon several occasions the crew desired the captain and officers to give up the ship."

"Don't give up the ship!" is a famous watchword, and the principle involved is held as firmly in the British mercantile marine as in the Royal Navy. No bulldog captain who nailed his flag to the mast and fought till not a stick would stand, ever displayed more resolution and tenacity of purpose than this quiet-faced, plain, merchant skipper out of Yarmouth. George Churchill had not the slightest intention of giving up his ship, even when he had still stronger inducements to abandon her. Such a case as the *Thomas E. Kenny* abandoned at sea is still remembered to the disgrace of the captain. The skipper of the *Noel* left her on the rocks after thirty-six hours labour, but she was afterwards salvaged, and it broke his heart. Backed by his splendid nephew, and cheery, courageous, determined George Marshall, the captain of the *Research* persuaded his crew to remain at their duty, when their situation seemed desperate and their labour all in vain.

On January 10, in spite of the ocean's spite, Churchill prepared to send down his mainyard to form the stock of a new rudder. That he was ready to sacrifice this important spar shows the extremity of the *Research*.

"Why didn't he use his cro' jack yard?" the port warden asked.

Without the mainyard, the operation of "heaving-to," or stopping the ship's progress in the sea, would be well-nigh impossible. But the presumption is that Churchill knew what he was about. Three days later, the sixth rudder was constructed, and after several mishaps was got into place. Rudder number six was not carried away by the turbulent seas; it lasted until January 25, but it was not large enough to control the big ship effectively. Still it was better than nothing, and with its aid, Churchill the unconquerable navigated the *Research* towards Greenock.

Ever since the northwest blizzard struck her on the morning of November 27, the big timber-ship had been, as if abandoned by God to the will of the storm, solitary under wintry skies on the waste of waters; but now she was nearing the great traffic lanes between the old world and the new. Help was coming to her. On January 16, she spoke the ship *Empress Eugenie,* Collins, master, homeward bound from San Francisco. Across the stormy sea, whipping signal flags told her story. Both ships hove-to, and the boat of the *Research* rowed off for provisions. After such a long voyage, the *Empress Eugenie* could not have had much beef and biscuit to spare, but she did what she could to help a sister in distress. The very next day, the steamer *Palmyra,* Watson, master, also on her way to Liverpool from New York hove in sight and stopped to assist the crippled but unbeaten *Research.* From both these vessels, Churchill received "great kindness and friendly offers of aid." From both he accepted sorely needed supplies, but he refused to be taken off. An abandoned ship may mean a total wreck, but it may also mean big salvage, almost the value of ship and cargo. Pride, interest, duty forbade him to take the easy way out of his difficulties, and he stuck to his ship.

Besides the *Empress Eugenie* and the *Palmyra*, the *Research* received help from a third unnamed vessel. That the three friendly, helpful captains offered to take Churchill and his crew off his battered, leaking vessel with her crazy steering gear shows what they thought of her condition. In a raging storm, they had stopped to speak a wreck, which would never make port. At least the odds were decidedly against it. So the three ships went their several ways. When she reached Liverpool, the *Palmyra* thoughtfully telegraphed Lindsay & Co. that she had spoken the *Research* and supplied her with provisions. This was welcome news to the consignees, for they had long ago given her up for lost and were even then arranging for the insurance on the ship and cargo. It was, of course, during these three sea-parleys with their would-be rescuers that the crew wanted to abandon the ship. Starving and exhausted as they were, with little prospect of saving their lives, no one can blame the over-tasked foremast lads or withhold admiration from the iron-willed triumvirate of officers who refused to admit defeat.

Rudder number six could not be dislodged, but it was not working well. Churchill built a seventh on an improved plan. It was begun on January 25, and "after several ineffectual and heart-breaking efforts," was shipped two days later. The last line was hardly hauled taut, the rudder-stock was hardly home in the rudder-casing, when the stock broke and left it disabled. So rudder number seven is out of the saga.

By this time, the *Research* had clawed back from the neighbourhood of the Azores to the south of Ireland. The unbreakable resolution of the master was overcoming every difficulty. Churchill built another rudder, and on the first day of February, about 185 miles southwest of Cape Clear, it was shipped without mishap.

Practice makes perfect. These Nova Scotian handymen had learned from their failures and experiments. Seven is a complete, a mystical number. Poseidon was apparently satisfied with the sevenfold sacrifice. For rudder number eight was a success. With this triumph of perseverance, the luck of the *Research* changed; the wind became favourable and urged her up the Irish Channel. At Ailsa Craig, she fell in with a tug and accepted a tow. It was no disgrace. After a voyage of eighty-eight days under her own sail, with the aid of her eight improvised rudders, the *Research* had made port. She was hauled to the Wooden Wharf at the Tail of the Bank. Next day the *Glasgow Daily Herald* printed a brief item of shipping news:

"Greenock: Arrived, February 5th, *Research*, Churchill, from Quebec with timber."

That is all the landsmen would learn of the long duel between the spirit of man and the rage of ocean. And the man won.

122

At the Wooden Wharf, the *Research* was an "object of considerable curiosity." Well might she be! Very different she appeared from the trim portrait of her that hung in the owner's office in Yarmouth with every sail set and her flags flying. To the landsman's eye, she must have seemed a wreck. Mainyard, forward deckhouse, wheelhouse were gone, great ragged gaps showed in her bulwarks, her deck was cumbered with strange gear, and astern was her homemade rudder, but the costly hull was sound, and the precious cargo in the hold was intact. The insurance money would cover all repairs.

This tale has a happy ending. To the three unconquerable Nova Scotians came tangible rewards for their conduct as well as gratifying and well-earned words of praise. On March 10, 1867, there was a notable gathering of gentlemen in the underwriters' room of the Glasgow Exchange. They were convened for the purpose of presenting Captain Churchill and his two officers with various testimonials "in approbation of their conduct while in charge of their vessel on her voyage from Quebec to the

Clyde." Of the Glasgow Underwriters,—douce, home-keeping bodies,—not one was interested personally in the ship or cargo, to the extent of a penny-piece, but they knew how to admire pluck and perseverance. They put their hands in their pockets and bought a silver salver for Captain Churchill, engraved in plain terms with the record of his great exploit. This piece of plate is a treasured heirloom in the possession of his eldest daughter near Yarmouth. The chairman of Lloyds sent him a letter, commending his "indomitable perseverance." The Union Marine Insurance Company presented him with a gold watch and chain, and a purse of sixty sovereigns. Pious Mr. Euing, senior member of the underwriters, made the presentations and expressed the hope that these brave men would always be protected by Him who ruled the winds and "Who will bring all those who put their trust in Him, to a haven of enduring rest." And the Glasgow underwriters clapped their hands.

In his manly, seaman-like reply, Captain Churchill made them laugh by saying that "If shipmasters did not act as they should, underwriters required to increase the premiums, so that it came out of the owner's pockets in the end." Of course, he also said what every sailor would say: he had done no more than was required of him.

Churchill's achievement is unique in the annals of the sea, and to the end of his days, he was famous among his brother captains as "Rudder" Churchill. This honourable appellation was known even to the schoolchildren of Yarmouth. His pretty eldest daughter was teased when her schoolmates cast up the nickname to her, not knowing in her innocence that it was a greater honour and more dearly won than many a patent of nobility.

Nor did the services of the mate and the "invaluable" boatswain go unrewarded. To each was given a silver chronometer, watch and gold albert chain by the underwriters on the cargo, and a sextant in a case from the Union Marine Insurance Company.

Not many years after this memorable voyage, Aaron Churchill quitted the sea and like so many other able Canadians, found opportunity waiting for him in the United States. He went into the stevedore business, invented several labour-saving devices, founded the Churchill line of steamers out of Savannah, and made his fortune. It is told that behind his office he had a small room fitted up as a gymnasium to preserve his great strength. He never forgot his native Yarmouth. On the shores of Lake Darling, he built himself a summer pleasance, which he named "The Anchorage." During the Great War, he helped with sailor-like generosity to swell the county's subscriptions to patriotic funds and Victory Loans. When the United States entered the war, he put the Churchill fleet at the disposal of the government, and he gave his employees liberal inducements to serve their country. In a complimentary address, the Georgians likened him to General Oglethorpe, the founder of the colony. He lived out the allotted span and died in his bed, but he never forgot that bitter winter day under the counter of the labouring *Research*.

The Shannon *and the* Chesapeake, *triumphal entry into Halifax Harbour,*
June 6, 1813. Painting by an unknown artist.

THE GLORY OF THE *SHANNON*

For those faint hearts who fear that Britain is doomed to speedy decline, no better tonic could be prescribed than reading the naval history of the Great War[1]. From 1792 to 1815, Britain was fighting for bare life; she saved herself and she saved Europe by her unconquerable fleet. Everyone knows Nelson's name and the fame of Trafalgar and the Nile, but in those great and gallant days, there were a thousand little battles which have passed into oblivion.

For more than twenty years, British ships of war of all ratings were fighting almost daily in every sea. From the poles to the tropics, by day and night, at all seasons, in fair weather and storm, they were chasing their foes, or circling about them in black powder smoke, or hammering away yardarm to yardarm, or firing as they ran, or flinging the barefoot boarders, stripped to the waist and cutlass in hand, on the hostile decks in final desperate assault. But who knows, or cares, how the *Junon* beat off fifteen gunboats in Hampton Roads, or how the *Unicorn* ran down the *Tribune* in a chase of two hundred and ten miles, or how the *Amelia* battered the *Arethuse* in the tropic moonlight, with the muzzles of their guns almost touching? Such fighting will never be seen again. It passed with the days of sail, but the tradition is alive in the king's ships—dreadnought, cruiser, torpedo boat, and submarine—of the present day. The tale may be read at length in the neglected chronicle of James. There is not a

---

[1] The Napoleonic Wars

page in it but is calculated to foster pride of race and admiration for mere human courage and devotion to duty.

Of all these sea-duels, the most famous and memorable is the brief and terrible encounter between the *Shannon* and the *Chesapeake* off Boston lighthouse a hundred years ago. It is remembered for many reasons. Since Trafalgar, British ships had been regarded as invincible. The War of 1812 began, however, with a series of unexpected reverses at sea. Britain heard with incredulity, rage, and gloom that British captains had lowered their flag to the despised Yankees. The *Guerriere* and the *Java* had struck to the *Constitution,* and the *Macedonian* to the *United States.* Our ancestors felt as we felt when we learned that a British regiment with arms in their hands had surrendered in the field to a ragged Boer commando. Nothing could efface such black shame. Although these single-ship actions had no effect whatever upon the course and upshot of the war, their results depressed the British unduly, and naturally and justly elated the Americans. The British frigates were unlucky beyond doubt, but the Americans deserved to win because they had bigger, better built ships, because they paid more attention to gunnery, because they were bold and skilful seamen, and because they adopted the favourite British tactics of dashing attack and close action, while foreigners preferred the safer game of long bowls. As Lucas pertinently remarks, war is not knight errantry but business, and the surest way to defeat your enemy is to attack him in superior force.

Nowhere outside of England was the course of the Great War followed with more eager interest than in the good city of Halifax. In and out of the harbour passed famous ships which had fought under Nelson, and in the garrison had been quartered historic regiments which were to win fresh laurels in the Peninsula or at Waterloo. Officers of the army and navy mingled with Halifax society and married Halifax girls. De Quincey has told how the mail coaches carried the news of victory down from

London: "Oh, those were days of power, gallant days, bustling days, worth the bravest days of chivalry at least." When the news of a victory reached Halifax, the merchants hired a military band to play patriotic marches and loyal tunes on the roof of the market building, while they drank success to the British arms in their reading room opposite. The whole town would be illuminated and parties of young people would stroll about admiring the effect of windows full of candles. When the *Guerriere* was lost, the whole city was plunged in gloom. According to local tradition, the famous fight began in Mr. William Minns' bookshop, opposite the Parade. An old Haligonian remembered Captain Broke coming in with a walking stick in his hand and his epaulets setting firmly but carelessly on his shoulders, and saying, "Well, Minns, I am going to Boston." Boston Bay between Cape Ann and Cape Cod was a favourite cruising ground, for into that funnel poured a great tide of American commerce. Broke further told Mr. Minns that he intended to challenge the *Constitution*. He had been a frigate commander for eighteen years and had never encountered an enemy's vessel of the same class. Mr. Minns ventured to think that the *Shannon*'s eighteen-pounders would have no chance with the *Constitution*'s twenty-four-pounders. Broke replied that he intended to fight yardarm to yardarm and to depend on the devotion of his three hundred men, "each of whom, I know, will follow me to the death, and stand by me to the last." He would trust more to boarding than to the calibre of his guns. If this ancient Haligonian's memory served him aright, Broke had decided on his tactics before he left port. The *Shannon* was already famous for her many captures and for her captain's foible of giving his share—always the lion's share—of the prize money to his crew. By such treatment, by firm discipline, and by constant gun-drill, Broke had made his frigate perhaps the most effective fighting machine of her class in the navy.

Why did Broke mention the *Constitution* in his chat with Mr. Minns? He had many reasons for wanting to fight this particular frigate. Every post captain in the navy was burning to wipe out the disgrace of the British surrenders. "We must catch one of those great American ships...and send her home for a show," Broke wrote to his wife. But he had, I venture to think, a special reason for naming the *Constitution*. That vessel had defeated and taken two British frigates and Broke had been a member of the courtmartial held on young Captain Dacres for losing his ship. The courtmartial had been held on board HMS *Africa*, a Trafalgar ship, in Halifax Harbour. Only a naval officer can appreciate Broke's feelings. To sit in judgment on a brother in arms, whose sward has been taken from him, to know that your verdict may ruin his career is a severe ordeal. Dacres was freely blamed as a young and inexperienced officer in giving up his ship too soon. A Boston canard stated that he had fought two duels in consequence of his inglorious surrender. The facts are that he was the first to own defeat, and that he was unlucky. He fought his ship until every mast went over the side and the *Guerriere* was wallowing, an unmanageable hulk, in the trough of the sea. It was impossible to work her maindeck guns, the sea swilled through the open ports, and the *Constitution* simply chose her own position where not a gun of the *Guerriere* could reach her and proceeded at her leisure to pound her helpless enemy to splinters. Dacres himself was wounded and seventy-seven out of his crew of three hundred men were struck down before he gave in. It is difficult to see what else he could have done. Nonetheless to lose one's ship for whatever reason is black disgrace. There are no excuses in the navy.

On March 13, 1813, the *Shannon* and her sister ship, the *Tenedos*, weighed anchor, and, two towers of white sail, glided magnificently down the harbour past George's and Thrum Cap to the open sea. They went to cruise in company off Boston Bay, where homing prizes flocked thickest. It was their business and duty to destroy commerce, but what they hoped for was a battle with a couple of the four American frigates refitting in Boston harbour. They were to catch as many of the enemy's merchantmen as they could, make prisoners of their crews, and send the captured vessels with the minimum number of British sailors to navigate them to Halifax, there to be adjudged in the court of vice-admiralty. Prizes meant prize money, and "dashing in coaches," so service in frigates was much more popular than in the great three-deckers, the lumbering sea-wagons, whose business was to fight in a line with the like ships of the foe. Why frigates hunted in couples is obvious. One could support the other with her guns and boats if engaged near land and render aid if her consort in chase should get on shore. For more than two months the *Shannon* and *Tenedos* plied their trade, overhauling luckless merchantmen and bringing them to, or beating out to sea with scanty canvas when the cold easterly gales with rain and snow would force them on shore. The *Shannon* took some twenty-five prizes, which were destroyed because Broke would not weaken his crew by sending men off in them. The only exceptions he made were vessels belonging to Halifax, recaptures, and the property of British subjects, but he begrudged a single one of his three hundred, who "would follow him anywhere." He needed them all to work the ship and fight the guns.

On the first of May, the *President* and the *Congress* eluded the vigilance of the British cruisers, and favoured by the fog, sailed out to sea. Of the two that remained the *Chesapeake* was nearly ready for a cruise by the end of the month. Broke took a course which recalls the palmy days of chivalry. He sent Captain Lawrence of the *Chesapeake* a formal challenge to come out and fight him ship to ship. It was as courteous as an invitation to dinner or to spend a month at Brokehall. He gives the number of his crew and of his guns. He mentions that he is short of provisions and water. He has detached the *Tenedos* so no British ship will interfere with the duello.

This amazing letter begins, "Sir, As the *Chesapeake* appears now ready for sea, I request you will do me the favour to meet the *Shannon* with her and try the fortune of our respective flags." It ends, "Choose your terms—but let us meet."

This was not the only instance of a British captain trying to obtain "the satisfaction of a gentleman," in those days when a case of hair-triggers found a place in their portmanteaus as naturally as their razors. Sir John Yeo, of the *Southampton* challenged Porter of the *Essex*, and Parker of the "bold *Menalaus*" sent a message to Mallet of the *Atalante,* of the same tenor as Broke's. There seems to be some doubt whether or not Lawrence received the letter. At all events, he acted as if he had.

In the captain of the *Chesapeake*, Broke had a foeman worthy of his steel. Physically he was a giant; as a fighting captain he was bold and successful. Only a short time previously, in the *Hornet,* he had defeated the *Peacock* by the same methods that had proved so effective in other single ship actions: dashing attack, good seamanship, and first class gunnery. His word to his crew just before the fight began was "*Peacock* her." His ship was as fit as the shipwrights and riggers could make her. He had a picked crew. No vessel ever went into a fight with better chances of success. On this beautiful June day she began to spread her canvas at noon and as light airs prevailed, set all her sails, even her stunsails, and proceeded slowly down the bay, a stately white cloud with three large American flags ruffling from her rigging and a broad banner at the fore inscribed, "Sailors' Rights and Free Trade."

Under shortened sail the *Shannon* tacked to and fro, waiting for her adversary to close. Only one British flag flew at her mizzen. "Mayn't we have three ensigns, sir, like she has?" a sailor asked. "No," said Broke, "we have always been an unassuming ship." A number of pleasure boats followed the *Chesapeake* down the harbour to see the fight, and a dinner was prepared in Boston to celebrate the victory.

In those days of sail, there were two well recognized kinds of tactics. One was to open fire at extreme range, keep away, and aim at the rigging of the hostile ship in the hope of knocking away a spar and so render her unmanageable. The other was desperate "in-fighting," laying your ship as close as possible to the foe, grappling with him, and turning the sea-fight into a land fight by invading his decks with a rush of boarders. This was the favourite British method and the battle of the *Shannon* and the *Chesapeake* is a classic example of it.

It took all afternoon for the *Chesapeake* to reach the *Shannon*. At ten minutes to six the fight began, and all was over by five minutes past. This most famous fight lasted just a quarter of an hour.

You are to imagine the two fine frigates drifting slowly nearer and nearer in the lovely June weather, both heading east and sailing on parallel lines. On both every gun is loaded and run out; around each gun is grouped each gun crew, all along the low, dim perspective of the maindeck; the powder-monkeys are ready to carry cartridge from the magazine; cutlasses and boarding-pikes are laid out for the boarders; down in the cockpit, the surgeon and his mates are waiting with lint and bandages, saws and knives for the first wounded man who will be eased down to them. Naval gunnery was not a fine art in the old days. The *Shannon*'s maindeck guns were loaded alternately with two round-shot or with one round-shot and one grape all along her broadside. Imagine, if you can, the effect of these missiles fired into a wooden ship, at pistol-shot range, when you could see the faces of the men you fired at.

133

Broke had made his little speech before action to the *Shannon* from the quarterdeck. They were to kill the men. "Go quarters and don't cheer," he ended. The *Chesapeake* was now close; her crew gave three cheers, but it was still all over the British ship. As the bow of the overtaking *Chesapeake* reached slowly past the stern of the *Shannon* the captain of the fourteenth gun pulled his lanyard, the gun roared, and the shot was observed to strike near the enemy's second port. Then a bow-gun spoke; then the rest as fast as they could be fired, but there were only two broadsides fired. Now Broke's gun-drill told, and the effect of the well served guns at close range was deadly. The two frigates were shrouded in smoke. Slowly the head of the *Chesapeake* turned away and her stem ground along the *Shannon*'s side towards the bow until she was checked by the fluke of the *Shannon*'s anchor catching in the *Chesapeake*'s quarter port. In this position she was raked by the British guns.

This was another critical moment of the fight. The *Shannon*'s boatswain William Stevens had fought under Rodney in the Battle of the Saints and was now nearly sixty years of age. As the ships scraped, he went over the side and began to lash them together. He had his left arm hacked off by repeated sword-cuts and he was mortally wounded by musketry, but his lashings held long enough to make a bridge for the boarders. Broke, who had run forward, saw the Americans flinching from the quarter-deck guns, and calling, "Follow me who can!" stepped from the *Shannon*'s gangway rail to the *Chesapeake*'s aftermost carronade and so to her deck, with about twenty men from the forecastle. He had ordered the maindeck boarders and quarterdeck men to be called away, but he did not wait for them. Not a man or an officer was to be seen and the British swept forward over the bloody deck. At the gangways, there was some slight resistance, but the Americans were driven below, or they flung down their arms. Never was a speedier triumph.

134

Two unlucky incidents took place almost at the same instant at the opposite ends of the captured ship. The boarders had swept the deck clear of the foe in a few breathless minutes and reached the forecastle. Here the Americans threw down their weapons. Broke placed a sentry over them and turned to give orders to fire into the *Chesapeake*'s main-top, when three of the Americans who had surrendered snatched weapons from the deck and rushed at him. The sentry's shout warned him of his danger. He wheeled about, parried the midmost man's pike thrust and wounded him in the face, but one of his comrades stunned

Broke with the butt-end of a musket and the other laid his head open with a cutlass. His assailants were at once cut down by the furious "Shannons," but the wounded captain was never the same man again.

As the first lieutenant Watt followed Broke over the side with the quarterdeck boarders, he was shot in the foot and fell on his knee. Quickly rising he gave orders to fire one of the *Shannon*'s six-pounders into the mizzen-top, whence he had received his wound. According to Dr. Akins, a sailor had run on board with a small British flag on a boat-hook. With his own hand, Watt lowered the stars and stripes from the mizzen-peak and bent on the British flag. In the tangle of colours and halliards, he bent on the British flag below, instead of above, the American, and when he began to haul the two up, the American was uppermost. To the men of the *Shannon* peering through the thick smoke, this could have only one meaning, and they fired at the dim figures on the quarterdeck with deadly aim. A grape-shot carried away the top of Watt's head and killed four or five of the men with him. Then the flags were hoisted properly. The Americans below surrendered and the fight was done.

Two broadsides and a swift rush of boarders and the battle was over. Before the following yachts could realize what had happened, the American crew were in the very handcuffs they had laid out on the deck for the British, and the two frigates were making sail for Halifax. This was the most murderous fight in the long annals of single-ship actions. The victorious *Shannon* lost eighty-three killed and wounded and the *Chesapeake* one hundred and forty-six. Almost one man out of every three engaged was struck down.

Sunday, June 6, 1813, was a very beautiful day in Halifax, a day long remembered. During the morning service, someone came into St. Paul's, whispered to a friend in the garrison pew, and hastily left the church. An observer thought of fire and followed him. Soon the church was empty. All the city was on the wharves and house-tops cheering like mad at a procession of two

135

frigates coming slowly up the harbour past George's Island. The first was a "little dirty black ship," said Aunt Susan Etter, who saw them with her own eyes as a girl of thirteen, "and the other was a big fine ship." The first was the *Shannon*, her paint sadly weathered by three months cruising, and the second was her prize, the *Chesapeake*, still fresh and glittering from the Boston shipyard. As they passed, the spectators observed that the decks were being swabbed and that the scuppers were running red. The bands played and the ships in harbour manned their yards in honour of the victory. The two vessels anchored near the dock-yard and at once began to send the wounded ashore.

No visitors were allowed on board the *Shannon*, for the captain's head wounds made quiet imperative, but two eyewitnesses have left on record what they saw 'tween decks of the *Chesapeake*. Both were boys. One writes:

> *She was like a perfect charnel house. Her main deck from forward of the mast to the extreme stem of the vessel was covered with hammocks, in which lay the wounded, the dying, and the dead, each hammock having a cord or rope suspended to it from the roof of the deck, so that the poor fellows might lay hold of it and ease themselves up....Very many...lay writhing in their wounds.*

The other boy was Thomas Chandler Haliburton, the creator of "Sam Slick." He gives more details:

> *The deck was not cleaned (for reasons of necessity which were obvious enough) and the coils and folds of rope were steeped in gore, as if in a slaughterhouse...She was a fine built ship and her splinters had wounded nearly as many as the Shannon's shot. Pieces of skin and pendant hair were adhering to the sides of the ship, and in one place I noticed fingers protruding, as*

if thrust through the outer wall of the frigate, while
several of the sailors to whom liquor had evidently
been handed through the portholes by visitors in boats
were lying asleep on the bloody floor, as if they had
faded in agony and had expired where they lay.

Great honour was done to the victors. The Halifax merchants presented Broke with an address and a piece of plate. The home government promoted him, gave him a pension, and made him a baronet. He never entirely recovered from his wounds. Aunt Susan Etter remembered the white handkerchief he wore about his head in the streets of Halifax. He quitted the service and spent the afternoon of life as a country gentleman, devoted to his family, tending his estate, reading Horace, and going to church. Incidentally, he underwent a formal courtmartial for altering the equipment of his ship. The second lieutenant, the Halifax boy who brought the vessels safely to port, who was never out of his clothes and hardly slept during those six critical days, became commander and rose to be Sir Provo Wallis, admiral of the fleet. He died in 1891, more than a hundred years old. Honour was also done to the dead. Lawrence, who brought his ship into action so handsomely, as Broke wrote, died of his wounds on the way to Halifax. Haliburton saw his huge frame lying on the quarterdeck of the *Chesapeake* with the stars and stripes for a shroud. His last words, "Don't give up the ship!" will never be forgotten by his countrymen. On Tuesday, June 8, 1813, his body was buried in old St. Paul's cemetery. His remains, says Murdoch, "were landed under a discharge of minute guns, at the King's Wharf, from whence they were followed to the grave by his own surviving officers, those of H.M. navy and army, and many respectable inhabitants of the town. On the American flag which covered the coffin was placed the sword etc., of the deceased, and the pall was supported by six captains of the royal navy. A military band attended, and 300 men of the 64th regiment fired three volleys

137

over the grave. The funeral service was performed by the rector of St. Paul's Church. Nothing could be more solemn and impressive than this procession, from its landing at the King's Wharf to the close."

The lasting glory of the *Shannon* does not lie in the careful organization of victory, nor in the success of her deadly onslaught, nor even in wiping the stain from the tarnished flag. It is found in the spirit of her commander, who obeyed "the imperious call of honour." Broke was a rich man, happily married; he might have spent this life in ease and comfort, but, "Surely," he wrote, "no man deserves to enjoy an estate in England, who will not sacrifice some of his prospects, either by actual service, if possible, or at least by example of zeal and voluntary privation in her cause."

"The Sarah *Stands By." Sketch by Donald Mackay, from* Tales of the Sea.

THE *SARAH* STANDS BY

In the month of January, 1850, the city of New York went wild over a plain master mariner from Yarmouth, Nova Scotia. Wall Street, the mayor and corporation, the press, the ladies, and the populace of Gotham showered attentions upon him. He excited the interest of even such august bodies as the senate of the United States and the house of representatives. His fame extended far beyond the bounds of America. "Solid pudding" as well as "empty praise" were his in no stinted measure, and then he went his way, and New York knew him no more. The excitement passed and is forgotten as well as the reason for it, but the memory of brave deeds well done should not be allowed to perish from the world for lack of a faithful chronicler. This is the tale of two ships and two captains; one of the captains was a man.

The saga begins in the river Mersey, on October 23, 1849, with the sailing of the smart American packet-ship *Caleb Grimshaw* from Liverpool for New York. Grimshaw is an old Liverpool name. A Robert Grimshaw was captain of the *Spy* privateer in 1757. Caleb Grimshaw & Co. was a Quaker firm of ship's agents; the head of it used "thou" and "thee" in a letter of remonstrance to *The Times,* of which more anon. Evidently this vessel had been named out of compliment to him when she was built two years before in a famous New York shipyard, and she belonged to the firm of Samuel Thompson & Nephew. A new, able, well-found ship, she represented the last word in naval architecture, used as a model for the class praised by Dickens in *American Notes* as "The noble American vessels which have made their packet service the finest in the world." Her captain was William E. Hoxie, who had been in the service for twenty years, reputed as both competent and trustworthy. He was a tee-totaller himself and sailed his ship on temperance principles. His eldest son, twenty-two years of age, sailed with him as first mate, and he had his wife and a younger child on board. An American packet of this day measured about a thousand tons, and between decks, with the rudest accommodations, this particular vessel carried 427 steerage passengers, 100 of whom had only a month to live. Some modern steamers of ten thousand tons do not carry more. It was immediately after the cruel famine years, and the Irish were fleeing from their own stricken land in thousands and in tens of thousands. In the cabin were six first-class passengers. One of them was an unknown Englishman who had the gift of putting down in plain words what he saw taking place under his own eyes. This nameless eyewitness is the chief authority for the tale; he lived through it. The *Grimshaw* carried a steward, a stewardess, and a doctor. Her crew consisted of eighteen men with four mates over them. Stowed below was a general cargo valued at half a million dollars. There were also one hundred tons of iron and between six and seven hundred tons of coal on the floor of the hold. To save passengers and crew in case of accident, the *Grimshaw* had only four boats, one at the stern, one on each quarter, with the longboat in its usual berth amidships, but these were considered an adequate provision. No vessel of the time carried more.

In the days of sail, there was a great difference in crossing the Western Ocean, according as the passage was eastward or westward. From America, the prevailing winds might rush a vessel across in fifteen days. Coming back from Liverpool to New York was another story. Head winds and calms often prolonged the voyage westward into weeks and even months. Sometimes an emigrant ship took a hundred days from port to port. The *Caleb Grimshaw* had the usual luck of westbound packets. By November 11 she was only about halfway across. To be exact, her position was 37° west, 41° north, which means that she was practically on the same parallel as New York and headed for her port of destination. Although it was winter, the neighbourhood of the Gulf Stream made the weather mild. The nearest land was Flores in the Azores, four hundred miles to the eastward. Sunday the 11th was memorable because, for the first time in almost three weeks, the *Grimshaw* had a favourable wind, and Captain Hoxie was able to set his studding-sails. Night came on. Though favourable, the wind was light and the *Grimshaw* with every stitch of canvas set, drifted along at the rate of two knots an hour. The emigrants were all below in their berths when, about nine o'clock, smoke began to pour out of the fore-hatch. Without a moment's warning, the calamity most dreaded by sailors had befallen the crowded emigrant ship: fire at sea.

At the cry of "Fire!" the shouted orders and turmoil on deck, panic terror seized the steerage. Well it might! Only the year before, the *Ocean Monarch* just out of Liverpool was burnt to the water's edge and 178 of her 399 passengers perished. That horror was fresh in all minds. Now the terrified men, women, and children poured up from below and rushed to the quarterdeck, the seat of authority, wildly imploring the captain to save their lives. Kneeling, lying down on the deck in the dark, drowning the officers' orders with shrieks of entreaty, the hapless emigrants made almost impossible the measures most needed for their safety. Some of them never reached the deck, but were suffocated by the smoke in their berths. Through the howling crowd, the officers managed to fight their way to the fore-hatch, the point of danger. On the forecastle just above it was a large force pump used for washing the decks. Two minutes after the alarm, it was manned and pouring a copious stream of water into the steerage. This force pump, as the ship's agents afterwards insisted truly, was the means of saving the ship, for the time being. First and last, it flooded the ship nine feet deep. Firebuckets supplemented the pump. Tons of sea water pumped into the *Grimshaw* sank her deeper in the water and almost destroyed her stability, but they did not touch the heart of the fire. Still the thick black smoke poured up from the fore-hatch through the sails and rigging to mingle with the black night.

After an hour of terrific exertion, with pump-brakes and buckets, the emigrants' quarters between decks were fairly well flooded, and still the smoke poured up the fore-companionway. It was plain that the fire was not in the steerage but deeper down, in the lower hold. One of the lower hatches was lifted by men stifling in the smother, and choking volumes of thick smoke poured up. The nozzle of the hose from the force pump was directed down the hatchway, fresh hands were put on the pump-brakes, but the fire was not checked. It only produced clouds of steam, and the heat was almost intolerable. "No human being could breathe between decks," said Captain Hoxie. Then young Hoxie volunteered to go down and discover, if possible, where the fire was. In a bowline, he was let down into the inferno of swift suffocation, but he was hardly below the combings when he sang out and was drawn up, almost insensible. In the few seconds he had seen the lower hold ablaze on both sides of the ship, abaft the chain locker.

His report must have spread throughout the ship as swiftly as the fire itself. Panic intensified. Order and discipline came to an abrupt end. While the captain's back was turned and he and his officers were battling with the fire, there was a rush for safety towards the stern of the ill-fated ship. Some of the passengers indeed volunteered to help the crew at the back-breaking, breathless labour of pumping, but others had to be driven out from among the women and children where they lay groaning and crying. Some others attempted to launch the port quarterboat hanging from the davits. Clumsy and panic-stricken, they

144

succeeded only in swamping her and drowning twelve of their number alongside. Panic spread to the crew of "packet rats." The man at the wheel deserted his post. He and the boatswain, the second cook, and several of the sailors put compasses, water, and provisions in the stern boat, lowered her without mishap, got in, and remained there in comparative safety for several days, towing behind the burning ship, and ready in an instant to cut the painter. They at least were provided for; passengers and messmates could shift for themselves.

If the emigrants had only hindered the movements of the officers and crew, if they had only hung back instead of helping with the pumps and buckets, the harm they did would have been negative. In their witless terror, they did far worse. They stove in the two huge water-tanks on deck holding eleven hundred gallons apiece and poured the contents down the hatchway. This is when a little pistolling would have presented far worse trouble later on, but Captain Hoxie and his mates were unable to prevent the suicidal work of destruction. Still the force pump clanked on and the bucket brigade was more thoroughly organized. This gave an opportunity for some of the crew to take in almost all sail and heave the vessel aback. Towards two o'clock on the Monday morning, the smoke seemed to be less in volume; the wild wailing and uproar died away, for the worn out passengers had fallen asleep on the hard deck wherever they could find a clear space, with only a few planks between them and the raging fire. Henceforward, they had to endure hunger and thirst as well as exposure and terror. All provisions were below and could not be got at without opening the hatches. Opening the hatches would mean the ship ablaze. Only by keeping air from the flames was there any hope of escaping swift destruction. Some of the emigrants did not taste a drop of water for ten days.

Monday was a day of comparative calm after the wild turmoil of Sunday night. When daylight came, a certain amount of order was restored. The starboard quarter-boat was lowered and three men ordered into her to keep her free. The port quarter-boat was baled out and three more sailors detailed to her. The stern boat remained towing with her occupants. These were plainly preparations for abandoning the ship. Anyone on board with a knowledge of arithmetic must have marvelled how three, or even four, boats could possibly save over four hundred and fifty persons. Eyewitness thought they might have accommodated one out of every ten. About nine o'clock, the longboat was hoisted out and passed astern. Mrs. Hoxie and the child were lowered into it from the stateroom windows, and the six cabin passengers followed. One was an old lady. Compasses, charts, oars, and provisions were also put in. Now all four boats were streamed astern. One of the midship pumps was got to work, and the sailors began to build a raft.

The scene at the after end of the *Grimshaw* must have been heart-rending. Eyewitness calls it "painful in the extreme. Some of the passengers rushed to the captain's stateroom, beseeching him to save them; numbers crowded around the stem where the second mate was lowering the ladies into the longboat; others were at prayers, while mothers and children, husbands and wives embraced each other and mingled their tears together."

Their fears were well founded. Before Eyewitness got into the longboat, the cabin floor was quite warm, and smoke was sifting through the seams of the deck. Two girls lowered themselves into the water by a rope hanging over the stern, although they were told they could not be taken into any of the boats. Still they clung together nearly exhausted, when room was made for them in the longboat.

Late in the afternoon came the abdication of the captain. One of the oldest rules in the rigid code of the sea prescribes that the captain shall be the last man to leave the ship. It holds good from the proudest dreadnought to the humblest fishing-smack. Rarely is it disregarded. But on Monday, November 12, Captain

William E. Hoxie betook himself to the longboat, amid wild Irish shrieks of,

"Oh, Captain dear! Save us! Save us!"

He assured his frenzied passengers that he would stay by them to the last, but his assurance gave them cold comfort.

The results of the captain's abdication were seen at once. So far as wind and weather were concerned, the situation remained unchanged. All Monday and Tuesday, the *Grimshaw* "lay-to" on a heaving, windless sea, with her four boats towing astern and the fire eating deeper into her entrails. On Monday, before the captain quitted his command, the sailors had constructed three rafts and hoisted one over the side. It was rigged with a mast and a small sail, and it was supplied with a barrel of pork, a barrel of beef, a little water, but no bread. Some twenty of the more energetic and more desperate among the emigrants got on it, and fearing that it would be overcrowded, cut the line which held it to the ship. Away it drifted before the wind to the eastward, to be swallowed up in the void.

Others of the emigrants were affected in a different way by the desertion of their official guardian. The instinct of plunder awoke. There must have been muttered plotting on the Monday, for when night fell, desperate men rushed the cabins, broke into all the trunks and boxes they could find and rifled them, just as the stewards of the *Scotsman* went through the staterooms, slashing open the passengers' luggage when she was wrecked in the Straits of Belle Isle. American packets were navigated on coffee, fore and aft, not rum. Perhaps the raiders were looking for food as well as spoil. At any rate, they found two cases of brandy and a few bottles of wine, not the property of the ship, but of the cabin passengers. The liquor drove the hungry men stark mad, and hell broke loose on the pitch-dark, filthy, crowded deck of the doomed *Grimshaw.* The only hope of saving the ship and the lives of all on board lay with young Hoxie and the loyal remnant of the crew, who still stood by him, and the homicidal

147

maniacs got hold of two guns and tried to kill them. Hoxie and his trusties met them with their bare fists. They overpowered the howling lunatics who carried loaded guns, wrenched them out of their hands and flung them into the sea. They armed themselves with pistols and bowie-knives and "kept the infuriated savages at bay," until the brandy died out of them, and they sank down exhausted. All through this riot in the dark, while young Hoxie and his loyal followers were fighting for their lives, not a man in the towing boats lifted a hand to help them. How long the riot lasted is not known, but at last it came to an end, and once more the peace of utter weariness settled down on the burning ship and her human stye.

An American "bucko" mate is a hard man to kill. On Tuesday morning, young Hoxie came off in one of the boats with some provisions and a small tin of water for his father and the other occupants of the longboat. He reported a terrible night.

148

Tuesday the 13th passed quietly. The boats brought off some mattresses and leaves of the cabin table, which were laid along the bottom of the crowded longboat. She was so leaky and shipped so much water that two men were kept bailing, day and night. Evidently the longboat had made many voyages secured amidships upside-down and was no longer seaworthy.

On Wednesday the 14th, the wind blew fair for the Azores, but the *Grimshaw* remained stationary. In the afternoon, the crew found a barrel of flour, and during the night of the 14th–15th, one man on board the *Grimshaw* did his duty, the first cook. All night he was busy in the galley baking. Captain and Mrs. Hoxie and all in the longboat had been subsisting uncomfortably enough on "cake, pickles, and cheese taken from the cabin." They found a cask of the cook's fresh bread very welcome.

About nine o'clock this morning, the crew made sail on the *Grimshaw.* Still burning, with nine feet of water in her hold, the smoke still coming up the forward hatch, she went lurching off vaguely in the direction of New York. This was an error in judgment, plain even to the intelligence of cabin passengers, and it was due to Captain Hoxie, who still seems to have exercised control from his refuge in the towing longboat. Like the Duke of Plaza-Toro, he led his regiment from behind. When night came on, the *Grimshaw* was hove-to by his orders, for the longboat was in danger of swamping. An old sail-cover was passed out from the ship and nailed over the boat like a tent or awning. It kept the seas from breaking over the side. On Thursday, at the entreaties of the mates and the crew, Captain Hoxie allowed the course of the *Grimshaw* to be altered, and she was headed for the Azores. By noon she had run eighty or ninety miles to the eastward recovering lost distance, and at night she was again hove-to.

On Friday, at dawn, the hard-worked remnant of the crew made sail again. About nine o'clock, it fell calm and the cabin passengers, wearied with their cramped quarters, misery, and constant danger in the longboat, "where we had lain four days and nights side by side without being able to change our positions and completely wet through," got back into the ship. Captain Hoxie remained where he was. An hour later, the lookout sighted a dim shape wavering on the far horizon,—a sail! It meant reviving hope to all on board; it might mean rescue and life preserved in dire extremity. The course of the *Grimshaw* was altered in order to cross the stranger's track, but there was little wind and progress was slow. To try and overtake her, the second mate put off in one of the boats, with five hands. They had a long, hard row which lasted till nightfall. All eyes on the *Grimshaw* were turned towards the strange and indifferent ship, with what hopes and fears. At the end of two hours more, they were able to distinguish the rig and course of the distant vessel. She was a barque standing west by north, on the road to America and away from the Azores. For two hours more the *Grimshaw* followed her, till hope of rescue was as good as dead. It seemed as if the stranger meant to avoid the ship in distress, and young Hoxie put his vessel on her former course eastward.

But keen eyes were watching the manoeuvre from the stranger's deck. As the *Grimshaw* came about someone on board the distant barque spied the stars and stripes fluttering, union down, in her main rigging. Until that minute, the flag was invisible from the stranger's deck. No doubt it was the captain himself who read the signal of distress through his big brass telescope, which he was destined to put to a very different use. Instantly he wore ship and began to follow the *Grimshaw* to the eastward. Hope revived. In an hour's time, she was near enough to speak and give young Hoxie necessary information in the curt speech of the sea: "—*Sarah*,—of Yarmouth—Nova Scotia—Cook, master—timber ship—in ballast—from London—homeward bound—will stand by" and the first mate barked back the plight of the *Grimshaw*. Cook directed him to keep the *Sarah* company. Both vessels would burn lights to guide each other. So they stood on together to the eastward.

The master of the *Sarah,* David Cook, was a typical Yarmouth County skipper. For three generations, the Cooks had followed the sea. Ephraim the grandfather came to Yarmouth in 1762. He was the first Englishman in the county, and though he lost a leg as a young man, he sailed vessels and founded the fishing industry in that part of the province. To the Yarmouth children, he was *the* Captain Cook who had *not* perished in the Pacific. And Ephraim begat Caleb and Manasseh, and Caleb begat Caleb the second, and David, our hero, and Nehemiah and Amos. The Cook pedigree reads like a chapter in Genesis. In all, there were four-and-twenty master mariners of this one stirp. Are not their names written in the book of the *Chronicles of Yarmouth* by George S. Brown? The Cooks were men of tried ability, for fools and weaklings do not rise to the command of ships. David Cook was a tall, handsome, athletic, young man, not long married. In this crisis he proved true to the splendid traditions of a seafaring race.

After the five days of merciful calms and light airs, a change of weather was due. Captain Cook prepared for the emergency by shortening sail. He took in his courses and top-gallant sails, and double-reefed his topsails. The expected gale came. That night it blew hard with frequent squalls. Before night fell, however, the *Sarah* had picked up the second mate's boat, and taken the sailors out of one of the quarter-boats. Captain Hoxie, his wife and child, the steward, stewardess, and doctor were also rescued from the miserable, leaky longboat, though they had a narrow escape from drowning while getting on board the *Sarah* in the dusk of the stormy November day. The wind and sea were getting up. It was impossible to take any more persons off. Eyewitness was among those who remained on board the *Grimshaw* in the night of terror which followed.

That the *Sarah* was proceeding under storm canvas shows what she expected. The emigrant ship followed as best she could, at a slower pace. The three boats towing astern were swamped and lost; and the stem was dragged out of the rotten longboat. Weighted down with the nine feet of water in her hold, the *Grimshaw* rolled and wallowed frightfully in the heavy sea. When she rolled to one side, the tons of water below would hold her down on that side for minutes that would seem ages. Then she would recover slowly and the sickening roll to the other side would begin. At every roll, the deck must have been almost at right angles to the plane of the sea. And this rolling continued all night. Eyewitness says:

"Every moment we expected to go down; the ship rolled in a frightful manner, dipping her studding-sail booms quite under water, while at every roll, the seas came in on the quarterdeck and even into the wheelhouse."

These restrained words express faintly the feelings of the cabin passengers on the quarterdeck. The terror of the three hundred poor creatures, men, women, and children, half-naked, drenched, famished, parched, exhausted, unsheltered on the main deck can be imagined. Holding onto whatever they could clutch for dear life, they must have been flung from side to side, into the scuppers, the whole night long. And among them were at least two expectant mothers whose time was near. They could feel the whole deck working under them, six inches each way, at every roll. The whole interior of the hull was on fire. No one knew when the flames might burst out. To make their despair complete, about three o'clock in the morning, they lost the faint twinkle of the *Sarah*'s lights. On board the *Grimshaw,* there was not an aid to navigation left, no chart, compass, sextant, chronometer; but somehow, by some seaman instinct, young Hoxie managed to navigate his vessel and keep her on her course. She was a new vessel and must have been staunch and well rigged to survive such a racking. Some principle of buoyancy kept her afloat, and she lived through that night. When the long expected dawn came, the anxious watchers in the *Grimshaw* saw to their great joy the faithful *Sarah* five or six miles ahead, pitching and tossing on the stormy sea.

Still they misjudged her, not knowing Captain David Cook. They thought he was going to desert them, as the barque sailed on ahead and made no sign. Nothing was farther from the master's mind. About two o'clock, the sea had somewhat abated, and the *Sarah* was hove-to. Two hours later, the *Grimshaw* came up with her friend in need, and also hove-to. And now another Yarmouth man comes into the saga, James Coward, first mate of the *Sarah*. The surname is a mistake; never was a more complete misnomer. The captain's place is always on board his own ship; he is the directing will, and the first mate is his chief executive to put the captain's will into effect. Courage is assumed as a first axiom and taken as a matter of course. He cannot do his work without it. Like that mirror of all seamen, Francis Drake, the first mate is "first at every turn where courage, skill and industry are wont to be employed." Now under James Coward's direction, the *Sarah*'s two boats were lowered, pulled over to the waiting

Grimshaw, loaded with their human freight, and conveyed safely to the deck of the rescue ship. It was a task calling for cool judgment, swift action, and professional skill. Women and children came first, for that is another ancient rule of the sea. To get them safely over the side of a rolling vessel into a small boat pitching and tossing alongside is no easy task. But Coward and his men did it. With the male emigrants there was no special problem; they could let themselves down by means of ropes. This women could not do, lacking the strength and the nerve; they had to be lowered in slings. Rescuing the children was harder still, for neither method was applicable to them. But trust sailors for ingenuity. The sixty-one children and the six small babies were done up in bags and so passed down the side of the *Grimshaw* and up the side of the *Sarah.* One of the marvels of this tale is the saving alive of so many children. Between three o'clock and dark, the *Sarah*'s two boats transhipped 133 persons, including most of the women and children, without a single mishap. Amongst them were the cabin passengers, including Eyewitness. Then the *Sarah* hoisted in her boats, and shaped her course for Flores, showing a light in her mizzen cross-tress as a guide to the *Grimshaw* through the darkness.

All Sunday the 18th, the two vessels continued on their course, but they could not communicate with each other. The weather was too wild. To the sufferers on board the *Grimshaw,* Saturday, Sunday, and Monday must have been an endless abyss of misery, deep opening into a still lower deep. The terrible wallowing roll of the vessel one-third full of water, the heavy swing to port and starboard, the painfully slow recovery went on without cessation and threatened to rack the masts clean out of her. The wonder is that she did not turn turtle or be thrown helplessly on her beam-ends. Thanks to her strong construction, she kept afloat and staggered on to eastward in the *Sarah*'s wake. Sleep, food, drink, rest were strangers to the *Grimshaw;* exhaustion, hunger, thirst, fear possessed her. But weakened as they were by want of food and ceaseless labour, young Hoxie and his faithful handful stuck to their task. They could not get sail enough on their ship to keep up with the *Sarah,* and on Sunday afternoon they lost sight of her altogether. That night the *Sarah* lay-to and kept a lantern burning in the rigging. On Monday morning, she sighted the *Grimshaw* nine miles away on the lee bow. By ten o'clock the *Sarah* had come up with her and swept by within hail, telling her to follow. Piteous cries of "Water! Water!" rose from the deck of the emigrant ship, but nothing could be done for them. The weather was still too wild to permit of sending off boats, and the *Sarah*'s supply of water was scanty enough. The *Grimshaw* wallowed along in her wake as best she could, under fore and main topsails, foresail and fore topmast staysail. To and fro swayed the masts, for all were loose in their steps. The mainmast could be plainly seen swaying several feet from side to side, as the ship rolled and plunged through the stormy sea, but still it stood. From the fore topgallant-yard ribbons of the lost sail streamed in the gale. In such plight, the *Grimshaw* staggered along eastward with her faithful consort, in the direction of the Azores.

154

Monday passed in the same way, and Monday night. On the Tuesday morning, the weather was still too wild to permit transhipping the remainder of the emigrants, but Captain Cook was at last able to render some assistance. He sent off a boat in charge of the *Sarah*'s second mate with seven fresh hands, nameless sailormen who volunteered to go. Quickly they spread more sail on the *Grimshaw.* With her mainsail, main topgallant and mizzen topsails set, she made better way, and the rocking masts still stood up. Back came the *Sarah*'s boat, with five spent sailors of the *Grimshaw*'s crew. They brought sad news. Twenty of the emigrants had died on the Sunday, and sixteen more on Monday night. That very morning four more had collapsed from hunger, thirst, and sheer exhaustion. In the ceaseless rolling, the poor creatures must have been flung in heaps from one side to the other and half drowned in the scuppers. There must have been sore bruises if not broken bones. And when the breath left the tortured bodies, the corpses would roll helplessly among the equally impotent living. And this hell lasted at least three nights and three days. Some emigrants had broken into the doctor's stores and drunk what they found there, laudanum probably amongst other drugs, and so passed away in a numbing stupor. Others were maddened and tried to kill young Hoxie. The tale is at its darkest when hope dawns. About eleven o'clock, Flores was descried as a dim cloud on the skyline forty miles to the eastward. Nine hours later the two vessels were safely under its lee.

It was now eight o'clock of a pitch black November night. Transferring passengers by night is no easy task, but the state of the *Grimshaw* and the weather conditions decided Captain Cook to attempt it, at all risks. At once the work began, and here again James Coward, first mate, comes to the fore. There would be strong arms at the oars of the boats, ropes over the side, and lanterns showing on the bulwarks of both vessels. To and fro between the stationary ships the *Sarah*'s boats plied for nine hours. Though all were faint with thirst and semi-starvation, though some of the women and children were in a dying condition, not one was lost. Between eight o'clock one night and five o'clock next morning, the work was done. One more dangerous job remained to do. The unguided *Grimshaw* must not be left adrift, a menace to navigation. Coward and his men made one last trip to the abandoned ship. They boarded her once more, and at the risk of their lives, knocked out the wedges from the heavy iron bars which secured the tarpaulins over the hatches. As soon as the smothered fire tasted air, the whole ship was one flame, but Coward and his boat's crew got away safely. In the black morning hour, the blazing ship lit up the ocean. From the *Sarah*'s deck, Eyewitness observed that the *Grimshaw* began to burn from the stern forward. With the removal of the hatches, the flames shot up the mizzen-mast, and it was the first to go over the side. The rickety mainmast crashed after it, before fire reached the topgallant sail. The last of the ill-starred *Grimshaw* was a dismasted flaming hulk drifting away two miles southwest of Flores.

The survivors were safe on board a staunch vessel in charge of as able a master mariner as ever trod a quarterdeck. A haven of refuge was not far away. But their troubles were not yet at an end. The *Sarah* was still smaller than the *Grimshaw,* measuring only 857 tons, absolutely without accommodations of any kind, except for her crew. All the rescued had to shake down on the open deck, with no shelter but the sky. Besides, no ordinary merchantman could possibly be prepared to feed a sudden addition of more than three hundred and fifty passengers. The *Sarah* had only six small casks of water and provisions for one week. It was at once necessary to put everyone on short allowance; the ration was half a pint of water per day, and half a biscuit morning and evening, just enough to keep body and soul together. Those who had been crying out for water when the *Sarah* passed on Monday could have had scant relief. It must have been during the confusion of the first day that an incident occurred, which was related to the present writer by Captain Cook's granddaughter. How discipline vanished on board the *Grimshaw* has already been told. Most of the crew stuck by the ship and backed their officers like sailors, but some behaved badly. It must have been some of these "packet rats" of whom the tale is told. Cook was walking the quarterdeck in the dusk with his big brass spyglass under his arm, concerned with the navigation of the *Sarah.* Below on the main deck, the emigrants were getting their half-pint of water per head doled out to them, when the captain heard a woman screeching. A single glance told him what was wrong. Four or five "packet rats" were trying to rob a woman of her allowance of water. He made one spring into the knot of struggling figures and laid out the ruffians on the deck with flail-like blows of his telescope. About the same time, he found that a priest had turned a woman out of her stateroom and taken possession of it

156

himself. Cook forgot the respect due to the cloth, and "gave him a beating," and reinstated the lawful occupant. If conjecture be admitted where there is no positive statement, this woman was probably the "old lady" cabin passenger in the *Grimshaw* and the stateroom was Captain Cook's own quarters. Nova Scotian skippers were famous (and notorious) for being able to command their own ships, and after these incidents, discipline prevailed on board the *Sarah*.

On the morning of Thursday, November 22, which is St. Cecilia's Day, eight corpses were dropped over the side of the rescue ship into the sea. Two women and six children had reached the *Sarah* and safety, only to die. Eight fewer persons however must have given little more room on deck. One hundred of the original number who had started from Liverpool a month before had perished. The remnant had saved their lives, and that was all they had saved. Some had not tasted water since the fatal Sunday when the fire was discovered. Their sufferings were extreme. No strong imagination is needed to picture their condition. Fortunately, the weather was not cold, owing to the nearness of the Gulf Stream. Had it been cold, says Eyewitness with conviction, many more must have perished.

157

About noon the wind died away, but later it came on again, and the overloaded *Sarah* headed for Fayal. She overshot her mark in the night, and when Friday morning broke, she was fifteen miles to leeward of it. The wind was dead against her, and all that day and the following night, she was slowly beating up to the island. It was not until the noon of Saturday, November 24 that she found anchorage in the roadstead of Horta, the port of Fayal. Her supplies, such as they were, had almost run out. Only two hundredweight of biscuit and two small casks of water remained for the needs of more than three hundred and fifty persons.

The *Sarah* rode safe in port with her rescued on board, and it might have been thought that at last, their troubles were at an end. But a new difficulty emerged. After defeating storm and fire, Captain Cook encountered a fresh antagonist,—human stupidity, against which, says the poet, the gods themselves fight in vain. In the struggle, he nearly lost his life, his ship, and all on board. When the port authorities came off to the *Sarah,* they informed Captain Cook that he must remain where he was, in quarantine, for five days. Reason they would not listen to. The special circumstances were not considered. Port law was port law. Every ship entering Horta must spend so many days in quarantine, and that was the end of it. So the *Sarah* remained in her first berth, held there by her anchors and even more firmly by Portuguese red tape. Efficient aid was promptly given by the British and American consuls. The first sent off necessities, bread and water; the second, the welcome luxuries of oranges and wine.

Sunday the 25th was a busy day for all on board the *Sarah.* She was worked a little farther into the harbour, but even this second berth was by no means safe. All day long, her boats plied between the ship and the shore, ferrying one hundred passengers to the lazaretto and bringing off barrels of biscuit and casks of water. In the evening, a small barque, the *Clara P. Bell,* sailed for New York. Her captain offered a passage to eight of the cabin passengers, but only two were allowed to go. The other accommodations were taken up by Captain and Mrs. Hoxie, the child, young Hoxie, who certainly deserved a rest, the second mate, the steward, and the stewardess. Before leaving, Hoxie chartered the *Sarah* to carry the surviving passengers of the *Grimshaw* to New York. He also wrote a letter to the agents, Caleb Grimshaw & Co. in Liverpool, apprising them of the loss of his ship. It is not an ingenuous letter. It tells nothing of his abdication or the splendid service rendered by his son. It is larded with pious phrases such as "The Lord be praised," which would appeal to a firm of Quakers. Its only good feature is enthusiasm for Captain Cook. "God bless him," "with a heart as big as Nelson's monument," are

158

two of Hoxie's references to him. So he departed in the *Clara P. Bell,* and now he is out of the saga.

"Wrecked in port," is not the empty phrase of a poet. It describes the fate of many a ship. It was almost the fate of the *Sarah* in the port of Fayal. The condition of the poor, starving, exhausted emigrants shelterless on her deck moved Captain Cook to "repeated complaints." At last, they had their effect and the wooden-headed customs house officials consented that quarantine should end on Tuesday morning. It might have been several hours too late. Tuesday morning might never have dawned for anyone on board the rescue ship. On the Monday, nearly one hundred more emigrants were taken ashore to the lazaretto, but more than that number still remained on board. The wind began to blow hard from the southwest and made the position of the *Sarah* dangerous. Foreseeing trouble, Captain Cook sent ashore for an extra anchor and chain-cable. It was sweated on board and let go. The wind increased to a living gale, and a third anchor was dropped. As night came on, the gale grew ever more violent, and all three anchors began to drag. Foot by foot, and yard by yard, the *Sarah* was forced back and back before the tempest, nearer and nearer to the dreadful lee shore. Few situations short of absolute wreck render the courage and skill of the seaman so futile as when his ship is dragging her anchors. He is at the end of his devices. There is nothing for him to do but wait and watch the danger becoming more imminent. Pitched and tossed and flung to and fro by the waves, the bulk of the *Sarah* tugged and jerked against the anchor-flukes in the bottom of the roadstead. At ten o'clock the strain proved too much for the best chain-cable; somewhere in its length, the stout links snapped, and the safety of the ship hung by the two cables that remained. For another hour and a half, the agony of apprehension continued, and in that time the *Sarah* had dragged five hundred yards nearer the line of breakers crashing on the shore and gleaming white through the blackness of the night. They were almost under the

159

stern. Death was staring them in the face. Again Eyewitness precises the situation:

"We thought it hard to perish thus, having escaped destruction so lately, to be sacrificed to those absurd quarantine laws; and harder still that Captain Cook should die a victim to his humanity in saving our lives."

What Cook himself expected is plain from his action. He left the deck and went below into the cabin to tell the ladies to dress themselves. He thought the *Sarah* would be on the rocks in the next few minutes. And then, in their extremity,—there was a lull; the vessel ceased to drag; the furious wind chopped round to the west; and they were saved. How narrowly they escaped was evident next morning, when the *Sarah* got her anchors up and moved farther into the harbour. On one, both flukes had been broken off. At the critical moment when the wind changed, the *Sarah* was held back from destruction by a single anchor. Such are the chances of life and death at sea.

The morning brought the end of quarantine, and security. The remaining passengers were put on shore, where they received every kindness and attention from the British consul. From November 27 until December 14, food and water for three hundred fifty passengers were taken on board and some sort of rude accommodations arranged for them between decks. The only incident recorded during the voyage to New York was two births. Two expectant mothers survived that fortnight of hunger, thirst, terror, and pain in the *Grimshaw* to bring forth living children. The voyage to New York lasted thirty days. On January 14, 1850, the *Sarah* reached port. Probably she took her place among the prows which thrust their bowsprits far over South Street, as in Bennett's famous picture. Dickens was impressed by this long vista of bristling spars.

The news of Cook's exploit preceded his arrival, and he received a royal welcome. He was lodged in the Astor House. A committee of the leading businessmen was formed to do him honour—"to mark their appreciation of his courage, gallantry and devotion." On January 17 he was called before the assembled merchants in the old Exchange in Wall Street to receive a resolution of thanks and welcome. It lauds his "humane and intrepid conduct" and repeats a phrase of Captain Hoxie's letter about his heart being "as big as Nelson's monument."

Cook was visibly affected by such testimonies of regard and replied in halting, commonplace sentences, still more eloquent than the most fluent Ciceronian periods:

"You make me feel proud.—You make me think—I have done a great deal—when I have done nothing—that was but my duty—and that my Maker did not require at my hands. I cannot give expression to my feelings at present—I am not in the habit of speaking in public. I feel most grateful for your kindness—and—I shall not soon forget it."

There is contemporary evidence as to the appearance and bearing of this typical Nova Scotian sea captain. The *Tribune* found him "exceedingly prepossessing. In height, he appears to be over six feet, is finely formed, erect, manly and dignified. He has the ruddy, English countenance and an open, pleasant set of features." The *Herald* report is not so specific. It calls him "a fine looking fellow. Just such a man as would do a good action for its own sake."

Plainly the hero looked the part.

The enthusiasm of the New York merchants did not evaporate in meetings and laudatory resolutions. With true American generosity, they raised a purse for him of eight thousand dollars. Of this sum, five thousand dollars went to Captain Cook himself, and he distributed three thousand dollars amongst the crew; seven hundred dollars to the first mate, James Coward; one hundred twenty-five dollars to each seaman; and one hundred dollars to each ordinary seaman and boy.

Nor was that all. New York itself, the mayor and corporation took official action. On Thursday, January 24, 1850, at two o'clock, there was a crowded meeting in the governor's room in the city hall. Along with a most flattering resolution, beginning "Resolved, That said David Cook is eminently entitled to the gratitude of the civilized world," the mayor presented the master mariner out of Yarmouth with an illuminated address and the freedom of the city in a gold snuff-box. Captain Cook was then brought before the assembly. He was received with hearty cheers. There was a rush to shake hands with him. The police from two wards, "with their staves of office," were needed to preserve order. It was in fact another "scene of enthusiasm." The ladies in an adjoining room were favoured with a sight of the hero "without being crushed or jostled by the other sex." This must have been when the New York ladies kissed him. The address, a triumph of Isaac Bragg's calligraphy in the frame of Verrocchio, which cost thirty dollars, and the snuff-box are preserved by Captain Cook's descendants in Yarmouth.

On June 20, 1850, the senate in which sat Webster and Calhoun voted a gold medal to Captain David Cook, but the house of representatives rejected the resolution. He did not therefore go without such a reward, for Lloyds presented him with their beautiful silver medal, *Ob Civos Servatos,* designed by Wyon the royal academician. It represents Leucothoe giving Ulysses the magic veil which keeps him safe. The reverse shows the oak-leaf garland the Romans awarded to a soldier for saving the life of a comrade. It looks as if there were little exaggeration in that phrase about "the gratitude of the civilised world."

Nor did Yarmouth fail to do honour to the hero. As soon as he returned from New York, there was a crowded meeting in the old court house in Main Street. The high sherriff presided, and Captain Cook was presented with an address signed by 235 leading citizens. Many laudatory speeches were made, and then the audience dispersed and the sailor went back to sea.

"The Thunderer" printed the narrative of Eyewitness on Christmas Day, 1849, and in a leading article, criticized severely the *Grimshaw*'s agents and Captain Hoxie. Grimshaw & Co. attempted a reply but with the usual result to those who venture to argue with a newspaper.

In 1864, Captain Cook was master and part owner of a small barque of two hundred eighty tons, built at Clementsport and named for his eldest daughter Louisa. On June 21, 1871, the *Louisa Cook* sailed from Shields for Philadelphia with a general cargo. It was her last voyage. On September 2, she was spoken in latitude 42°, longitude 65°, and was not again heard of. Her epitaph is a laconic entry in Murray Lawson's tragic list of the six hundred Yarmouth County vessels lost between 1777 and 1875.

His eldest daughter has sunny memories of her childhood home, of romps and games of hide-and-seek through the house with her tall, good-natured father, whose word still was law when he said "No!" She remembers his habit of walking in the garden, a child holding each hand, while he talked to himself about his day's business. "Another remembrance was prayers in the morning before breakfast. We could offer no excuse. We were expected to be there neat and tidy, chairs placed in a half circle in our old dining-room, and all listening quietly as my father read the chapter from the Bible; then prayers; afterward a cheerful breakfast with a full table as we were a large family."

In the old graveyard at Chebogue sleeps many a Yarmouth sailor, but many another rests in the ocean depths. No stone marks the grave of David Cook, but if ever a cenotaph is raised in his memory, it should bear the words he must have known: "He saved others—."

163

The Launberga, *South Maitland barque. Pen drawing from a picture postcard by* C. R. Wilcox.

THE CAPTAIN'S WIFE

Maitland is the Deserted Village of Nova Scotia. In the heyday of sail, its shipyards rang from daylight till dark with the clamour of saw and broadaxe and adze on hardwood, of mallet on caulking-iron, of hammer on trenail. At night, nine hundred men would be free to walk about the one long street. Maitland was the home port of famous ships and able captains. Here was built the great ship, the *W. D. Lawrence*, which made the Lawrence fortune in one voyage, the tragic *Esther Roy,* and many another staunch Bay of Fundy vessel.

Now the hamlet is shrunk and silent. Rarely does a human figure cross the street. The shore farms and the few remaining big houses look across the restless red waters of the Bay in their portentous ebb and flow, towards Economy and Masstown and Great Village, and beyond, to the blue range of the Cobequids. Sunset over these hills is like a gate opened in the Celestial City letting free the splendour of God.

The village smithy with the loft above it stands as it stood when Isaac Douglas forged iron work for Maitland vessels. He was a man of character whose sons followed the sea. Four of his daughters married Maitland captains and went around the world with their husbands. Margaret, the baby of the family, married the youngest son of "Squire" MacDougall, John Curry. He was named for the Presbyterian minister, who ended as a Hebrew scholar and professor of Old Testament exegesis in Pine Hill. That gives the measure of Maitland. Margaret Douglas was slender and tall, with exquisite hands and feet, a dark beauty, the clear red showing through her olive skin, eyes rather deep set, the chin firm, the mouth showing humour. Her old school-master remembers her as a bright, pretty, well-behaved child. In disposition, she was notably quiet and gentle, the sort of woman who would not say a harsh word of anyone, and she was a favourite with her own large family and many relatives.

So they were married, and in a few years MacDougall was in command of the big barque *Launberga* of nearly fourteen hundred tons. She was a masterpiece of his brother Adams, but she was also his ruin. He was three years in building her at South Maitland where the railway stands, which is a marvel to all who hear the tale. In 1892, when she was launched, wooden ship-building was already in its swift decline.

Now the story turns eastward. On Saturday, March 23, 1895, the *Launberga* was at anchor in Iloilo roads, near the low-lying, white-walled town with the old Spanish fort at the river mouth. She had carried a load of coal from Newcastle, N.S.W. to Manila. After discharging, she took in ballast and cleared for Iloilo to load sugar. At Manila, the hands had not been allowed on shore, but they were promised liberty at Iloilo, a promise which in the sequel could not be kept. Though they were the sweepings of Sydney, chiefly "Dutchmen," there had been no trouble with the crew, except with one Irishman, Pat Kelly. As soon as possible after making port on the Friday, Captain MacDougall went ashore to enter his ship at the customs. The British vice-consul told him his crew were not to have shore leave, because the last lot of sailors had run riot in the town and killed a native woman. MacDougall obtained a letter to this effect from the vice-consul. On returning to the *Launberga,* he called all hands aft and read the letter to them. They received the unwelcome news in silence and dispersed to their duty without a word. Two *carabineros*, or native policemen, well armed, were sent on board to prevent the sailors from going ashore.

All the Saturday, the crew were busy with whips and buckets, hoisting out the ballast into lighters alongside to make room for the sugar. Four bells struck. It was six o'clock, the end of the first dog-watch. Work was over for the day. Supper was ready cooked in the galley. Sweating, red-faced men lounged about the deck, while the ballast-lighter hoisted sail and began to move slowly away from the *Launberga*'s side. When a sailor makes port after a voyage, two things he must have. One is a drink. There was not a drop of liquor in the big barque. Curry MacDougall never carried it, even in the medicine chest. But a bumboat, knowing sailors' needs, had sneaked up to the bow with rum, and the sweating hands had drunk it. They were rather talkative and noisy. Beyond the widespread, green, misty paddy fields, a tropical sunset of violet, gold, and rose aspired to the zenith. All was peace at the end of the day's work. Then, without warning, the storm broke.

Captain MacDougall had gone forward to see that the lighter got clear away and then turned back to the cabin and supper. Amidships by the starboard main rigging, Mr. Bowyer, the first mate, James Evans, the second, and Tom Desmond, the boatswain were watching the lighter lazily fill and gather way. Two of the men just off duty, Brown and Shuman came aft to the end of the forward deckhouse and began talking *at* their officer with their backs to him in loud, rum-brave voices.

"What do you know about it? You old—" said one.

"You know nothing about it," said the other.

A regular Bluenose mate like George Crosby or Charlie Hunter would have stretched the pair on the deck the next second, but Bowyer was old and past his work. He made as though he had not heard their drunken insolence and walked aft toward the poop-ladder. As their officer retreated, Brown and Shuman faced round and shouted,

"You would not give us liberty."

"We will get drunk every day."

"Come on," shouted Shuman, "let's go for him," and they rushed him and knocked him down beside the maindeck capstan. Land, Goydlewski, Kelly, and Abrahams joined in beating him till Desmond pulled two of them off and gave the mate a chance to escape. Bowyer got as far as the foot of the short poop-ladder leading to the quarterdeck. Here Shuman assaulted him again but could not prevent him from reaching his poop, to which sacred precinct the foremast hands, awed by sea tradition, dared not follow. But only for a moment did they hesitate. Brown wrenched the door off the hen-coop, hurled it at the mate's head and missed. Shuman flung a lump of coal from the galley with better aim and hit him in the face. He crashed over the edge of the poop to the main deck where he lay as if dead. The six drunken sailors closed in, kicking the prostrate man and stoning him with lumps of coal….

168

Captain MacDougall had barely reached the pilot-house, or little porch at the forward end of the cabin, when he heard the riot and turned to see his first officer knocked off the poop and lying to all appearance dead. The men were beating him….

Mutiny, more dreaded than even fire at sea, had suddenly flamed up in the *Launberga*….The crew are many….The afterguard so few….Odds always against the officers….His wife—his two little children….He was unarmed….

He rushed down the companionway and through the mess room, where the table was set for supper. His wife in a white dress was standing with baby Annie in her arms, looking startled.

"Oh, what *is* the matter?"

"They've killed the mate. Where's my revolver?" and he hurried to his stateroom. In another minute he was back, pistol in hand. "It's not loaded. Where are the cartridges?"

"Here, sir, take mine. Don't wait!" and the steward, Robert Otto, a Shelburne boy, thrust his own six-shooter into his captain's hand. MacDougall sprang up the companionway, followed by the loyal steward.

Even the children in the mess room knew now what the uproar meant. The little Malay cabin boy snatched the carving knife from the table and started after his captain. Maggie MacDougall twisted it out of his hand, pushed him and four-year-old Fred into a stateroom, and turned the key. Then, always with baby Annie in her left arm, she ran through the inner room to the after-companionway and flew up on deck. The ballast-lighter was just passing the stern of the *Launberga* on her way to Iloilo. She was within easy hail.

"The crew have killed the mate," she shouted, "For God's sake, send the *gens-d'armes*. Quick! For God's sake! Do you understand?"

The lightermen's shout meant they understood. Margaret MacDougall ran round the cabin on the starboard side, clutching baby Annie, "to help the captain…."

A minute before, MacDougall had come out of the pilot-house and forward to the break of the poop in two strides.

"Get forward, men!" he thundered. "Do you want to kill the mate?"

"Yes," screamed Pat Kelly, "and you too, you—" and he headed the rush up the poop-ladder, his sheath-knife drawn. Close behind came Shuman, Brown, Land, Abrahams, and Goydlewski, the Pole, black and red, scowling faces, open, cursing mouths, all mad with rum, rage, and the taste of blood.

From the maindeck behind them, Desmond and Evans shouted:

"Shoot! Captain, shoot to kill!"

As the mutineers swarmed up over the poop, MacDougall gave back two or three paces and fired over their heads. But they were far beyond being cowed by any show of force.

Kelly, the foremost, struck savagely at MacDougall's head and laid his face open from the hair to the middle of the cheek. Red flooded the captain's face, blinding him. Red flooded his clothing….

Kelly struck again, madly....

The men were body to body. MacDougall fired a second time and Kelly went to the grimy deck as if pole-axed, flung on his back, with a bullet in his lungs. He lay bleeding and coughing blood. His shirt was smoking where the powder had set it afire.

The five others closed with the blinded captain, struggling to wrench the revolver from his hand. "Squire" MacDougall's sons were round-headed, round-barrelled men and dangerous fighters. Curry MacDougall fought for his life. Someone stabbed him in the neck. Another struck him on the back of the head with a lump of coal and felled him to the deck....

Why they did not end him there with a slash in the throat or a pass between the ribs is hard to tell. They did not want the will....

MacDougall struggled to his knees,—to his feet,—gripping his pistol,—and fought on,—blinded and bleeding. He was trying to work back to the pilot-house, and his enemies were trying to disarm him.

Up and down the five men wrestled, over the narrow area of the poop. Land got possession of the revolver at last and did two unaccountable things. Instead of emptying it into MacDougall's body, he stepped to the port side and fired a single shot. Then he ran forward, knife in hand, drove the *carabineros* into their room with threats of instant death, and fastened the door on the outside with rope-yarn.

Loyal Tom Desmond had raced up, weaponless, and flung himself between the knives and his captain. He threw his arms round MacDougall, offering his body as a shield, and shouting reason to the madmen. Otto also was in the melee, doing what a boy could to protect his captain. The mutineers dragged Desmond loose with curses....

"Damn you to hell, Tom....Get to hell out of this. We won't hurt you...."

"Let's finish the bloody swine...."

Gentle Margaret MacDougall, who could not say a hard word of anyone, saw and heard all this for two or three petrified seconds. Instinct, not reason, moved her. She rushed into the knot of would-be murderers and got her one free arm around her man.

"For God's sake, men, don't kill my husband," she screamed; and they gave back, hesitating, while you could count ten. Her unthinking, impulsive, natural action saved her husband's life.

Seizing the momentary respite by some miracle, she never could explain how, she and loyal Robert Otto dragged and pushed her husband inside the door of the pilot-house, though she was shut out and Otto was stabbed deep in the neck.

Shuman was the first to recover.

"Yes," he yelled, "and you too, you—"

He seized her and flung her with her baby to the deck. He struck her in the face and kicked her in the side. She was trampled underfoot. Desmond shouted, "Don't hurt the woman! Think of the woman and child!" His appeal touched one of the ruffians, Goydlewski, the Pole. He helped the battered, fainting woman, almost frantic with terror and pain, around the cabin to the after companionway, and somehow or other she found herself in the after-cabin.

Be it remembered to the honour of the common sailor that he also picked up baby Annie and put her in the companionway before joining his companions in their assault on the cabin. The poor mother thought her little girl had been killed or thrown overboard. Meantime, Desmond had bethought him of the armed *carabineros* and ran forward to their room. He undid Land's lashings, and knowing some Spanish, begged the representatives of law and order to come out and prevent murder, but they would not stir.

The death-wrestle on the poop had swayed to and fro over the narrow ten foot area where Kelly lay in his blood, cursing, groaning, coughing blood, and crying for help. The fighters had trodden on him.

"I'm dying," he cried. "Get a doctor—for Christ's sake—" At last, after Captain MacDougall got into the cabin, the mutineers heard Kelly's cries and paid heed to them.

"Signals!" he gasped. "Signal for a doctor—I'm dying—Get a doctor!—For Christ's sake." For a few moments, the would-be murderers turned aside to help their wounded leader.

Half stunned, panting, bleeding from two deep gashes, blinded by his own blood, MacDougall found himself in the mess room and made his way into the inner cabin or saloon. Otto fainted at the foot of the cabin stairs, where Mrs. MacDougall found him later in the night, lying in a pool of blood. To the inner cabin Mrs. MacDougall had already found her way. Bruised, dishevelled, badly shaken, she began at once to bind up her husband's wounds.

The two bolted and barricaded both doors. They must have expected nothing but death and known its bitterness. The clock against the bulkhead marked twenty minutes past six.

Overhead the uproar continued. The tramplings and outcries redoubled. The drunkards were fighting among themselves. They had broken open the flag-locker and strewn the contents all about. But no one knew which hoist would bring the doctor from the shore. They raged round the cabin like wild beasts, trying to break in, hacking at the windows with their knives, shouting obscene threats and curses.

"Come up, you — and show us what flags to hoist."

"Come up—"

"We'll cut your hearts out—"

'You haven't five minutes to live—"

They threw everything they could lay their hands on down the companionway. Mrs. MacDougall heard them going forward for axes to break through the skylight....

"We'll come back and finish the job."

And then, in their extremity, came unexpected relief. The minds of the raging drunkards took a new turn. Their victims had escaped, but poor Pat was dead or bleeding to death. As they could not find the signal for the doctor, the next best thing was to take Pat to the doctor. So they lifted the wounded man into the quarterboat and compelled the other watch to help them to lower it. Brown cut the falls, and next minute the mutineers were rowing for Iloilo, though they were soon diverted from their purpose.

The two in the cabin could hardly believe their ears when they heard the boat splash in the still water, and the sound of the oars die away. Then they were able to draw a long breath and attend to their injuries.

Bowyer, who was not so badly hurt as the captain and the steward, went off in a boat for a doctor. He had hardly gone before Captain Ned Hurlbert, of all men in the world, walked into the cabin. He was one of the MacDougalls' oldest friends. An hour after the mutiny began, his vessel, the *Bowman B. Law* of Yarmouth had anchored within one hundred and fifty yards of the *Launberga*. The mutineers had rowed out to her, and one had even climbed on board and perched on her rail till Hurlbert drove him off and went at once to the aid of his friends.

In another hour, the Spanish *gens-d'armes* arrived from Iloilo. Little Annie was found curled up unhurt and asleep by a water-butt forward, whither she had crawled in some unaccountable way.

The mutineers were arrested that same night, examined in Manila, and sent on to Hong Kong for trial. Shuman died of sunstroke in jail. The other four were sentenced to various terms of imprisonment. All the wounded afterguard recovered from their injuries, but the voyage back to New York was one long nightmare, with an incapable Lascar crew and Mrs. MacDougall's nervous breakdown. Curry MacDougall was never the same man again, and he carried the mark of Kelly's knife to his grave.

W. N. Zwicker, *schooner and rescue ship*, 1902

THE LUNENBURG WAY

The four-masted schooner *Joan Keilberg* was lying alongside the grimy wharf, having just made Halifax in seventy hours from Flushing, N.Y. with a load of coal. Her captain, "Jimmy Leander" Publicover, knows how to get the most out of his handsome, speedy, nine hundred ton vessel. Five men out of Lunenburg suffice to handle her. His father, Leander, Mark I, aged seventy-six, sails with him as mate and gave a hint how the *Joan Keilberg* earned profits for her owners in the lean years, when she carried pulpwood, summer and winter, in all weathers, from Mahone Bay to New York. "Been sailin' two years and never tied a reef-p'int in her yet. May have eased the peak-halliards," he conceded.

Captain Publicover was discovered in his ample cabin making a toy schooner. Mrs. Publicover was entertaining some friends. Several children were playing about, but Billy, the eldest, aged sixteen was living in the fo'c's'l, learning his trade like his father and his grandfather before him. Captain Publicover is a little, slight, dark, neat-footed man with a high, arched, aquiline nose. His expression is close, unsmiling, suggestive of nerves and anxieties. He could not be described as a willing witness when he told of his experience with the water-logged *Tilton*. The facts had rather to be dragged out of him. One would almost think the gold watch and chain awarded him officially by President Woodrow Wilson in the name of the great republic for saving the lives of seven American soldiers involved some sort of scandal. But the Lunenburg way is not effusive.

In December, 1912, Captain Publicover was bringing the tern schooner *W. N. Zwicker* of 398 tons back from New York to Ingram Docks, Nova Scotia. His brother Charles, aged eighteen, was mate, with three years experience, and the other seven were all Lunenburg boys of the finest race of sailors afloat. On Friday, December 20, the *Zwicker* was forty miles east-northeast of Cape Cod, homeward bound, in a gale from the northwest with snow squalls and a heavy sea. It was typical North Atlantic winter weather. She was proceeding with reduced canvas, reefed mainsail, foresail, and staysail; the big spanker was safely stowed, as well as the jibs. At Flushing, the *Zwicker* had been swept clean and was navigating without an ounce of cargo or ballast. Most expert handling was needed to keep her from turning over.

"At nine A.M.," said Captain Publicover, "I sighted a tern schooner flying signals of distress, about two points off our lee bow and four or five miles away. She was heading south. She appeared as if hove-to, but through the glass I could see the gaffs. Her sails were blown away. I swung my vessel off and bore right down on her.

"We did not dare to go close enough to hail, but we could see seven men lashed to the spanker boom over the cabin-house, one after the other. They were sitting in the lee, of course, and got a little shelter from the waves which were breaking over her constantly.

"The decks were all that much under water." And he held his hand about four feet above the cabin floor. "Only the high bowsprit and the gaff were showing. The sea was breaking like over a ledge, and it was bitter cold."

A vessel with her decks under water, either water-logged or sinking, looks like a living person being lowered into an open grave. This was the plight of the tern schooner *Henry B. Tilton* of Isleboro, Maine, P. W. Sprague, master. Thirty-six years old, she had left Windsor, N.S., lumber-laden for New York a few days before but had encountered heavy gales. Her sails had been blown away, her seams had opened and let in the sea till she was water-logged, her bulwarks were smashed, her boats were gone, her stern was stove in and her whole deckload was canted forward. Every wave, as it encountered the solid mass of the submerged hull, broke and burst in a sheet of foam as high as the three mastheads. The crew could do nothing more but await death or rescue. Every wave buried and half drowned them, and the smothering agony was momently renewed.

The problem Captain Publicover had to solve was by no means easy. Rendering assistance and saving life at sea come as natural to the sailor as breathing. But vessels have been known to sail away and leave shipwrecked men to their fate, like the stranger who abandoned the raft of the *Regina*. Publicover had been wrecked himself, and saving life was nothing new to him. When the *Virginia* piled up under the cliffs of LaHave at night in the worst snowstorm in sixty years, he swung all his crew ashore, one after the other, over the bow with the jib downhaul. He was willing enough to attempt the rescue. But there were other considerations.

It was wild weather. The steamer *Florence* was lost that day; the big liners were delayed and reported the heaviest gales for years. Was he justified in risking his own vessel with all on board? She was light and rolled terribly. It seemed as if she might turn bottom up at every roll. Only the smartest handling could keep her from capsizing. Nor could she come near the wreck or launch a boat. Publicover might lose his vessel, his crew, his own life, in a vain attempt at rescue. For hours he laboured for a decision, torn this way and that.

"I reached to the northward, until twelve o'clock," said Captain Publicover, "so as to get away from the schooner and waited for the weather to moderate. If she sailed away or drifted away my conscience would be clear."

The seven frost-bitten, half drowned men, lashed to long boom, saw the strange sail come near enough to understand their desperate plight and then—desert them. Away she went to the northward till she was only an uncertain blur between the tumbling crested billows and the grey low-lying clouds. Their hearts died within them.

Then Publicover made up his mind. He wore ship, lowering his peaks and came about.

"I set the jib and came back quick. About three o'clock we came up with her again. I was going to try to take off those men, but nobody on board expected me to get through with it.

"I got my dory on the poop with tackles in the rigging to get her over quick. A lifebuoy, an iron bucket for bailing and the oars were lashed into her. When all was ready, I brought the schooner under the lee of the *Tilton*. I had to take chances every way, so I took 'em that way to start with. The sails were hauled down, and the wheel was hove hard down and lashed. I gave orders to the mate not to change her position unless I got to the leeward with the dory, in which case he was to run to the leeward of me and heave-to, which didn't happen.

"Then I called for a volunteer," because a shipmaster may not legally *order* a sailor to almost certain death, even if he himself leads the way.

"More than one came forward. Practically all. I picked Fred Richard, and made him understand if he drowned, my family wasn't to be blamed. I expected to be drowned myself."

That a captain should go off in a boat and leave his vessel in charge of the mate is clean against the ancient custom of the sea. It is unusual, almost unheard of. The captain's place is always on board his ship. Publicover was criticized for this action, but it is hard to see what else he could have done.

Fred Richard, aged twenty, new to the coasting trade and ignorant of danger, "jumped quick at the chance."

The two men stripped to their overalls and singlets, with their sheath-knives in their belts. They stood in the thirteen-foot dory as she hung in the tackles, steadying themselves by lifelines rigged over the side. Then as their cockleshell dropped into the turmoil of the waves, on the *weather* side the two, with the swift precision of acrobats, unhooked the tackles, slashed the rope-yarn that held the oars and began to pull like madmen away from the *Zwicker*.

"That was the hardest part," said Captain Publicover. They had to fight their way to windward over a quarter of a mile to the submerged hull of the *Tilton*.

"I called to the captain and told him I would try and save him if he would obey my orders. Which he was very glad to do. I told him to unlash one man at a time and get him down in the lee mizzen-rigging.

"So he did. It was smooth to leeward. We took two off the first time, one in each end of the boat. We drifted back about half a mile, but we daren't go alongside. They threw us lifelines from the schooner which we fastened round our passengers, and they hauled them on board same as a codfish."

For the first time, a faint smile crossed the captain's face. "Our fellows boused them on, same as you'd haul a shark. The cook had hot coffee for them as soon as they got on the deck."

"That first trip we were almost lost under the counter. They took the man out of the stern first and almost swamped us. But that learned us.

Then they set out on their second strenuous pull to windward, a longer pull, for the vessels were always drifting farther apart, and took off two more men. Four men in a thirteen-foot dory would bring her gunwale very near the water; there was urgent need for the bailing bucket, but somehow this miracle of rescue was performed a second time. A dory will live when a schooner will founder.

Then for the third time, in the failing light of the shortest day in the year but one, Publicover and Richard rowed back to the wreck and took off the three remaining men. Captain Sprague, of course, was the last to leave his vessel. If four men was a load for the dory, five seems impossible; but Lunenburg boys know how to handle a dory, so these two brought their precious freight to the safety of the rolling *Zwicker*.

"Then I said to Fred to send the bucket and lifebuoy and his oars and the thort on board. So he did. And we lost nothing. 'Now, Fred,' I said, 'you go in the lifeline.' The boys were getting anxious, for they didn't want me to go, and they thought they couldn't find the land without me.

"I watched for a good smooth. I made the end of one of the lifelines fast to the painter of the dory. The other I threw over my shoulder and grabbed my oars and the thort. By this time the dory was filled, and I was going up the side. We hoisted the dory in by one of the tackles, and the water spilled out of her. We lost nothing."

He was sweating in his overalls and singlet.

Expansiveness, as already noted, is not the Lunenburg way, but thrift is. There was no reason why a careful shipmaster who had earned the Victoria Cross three times in two hours should lose any of his gear, which costs money, and money is not easy to get in the coasting trade. After saving the crew of the *Tilton*, Publicover's mind turned not to thoughts of fame or self-congratulation, but to saving his dory and everything in it down to the movable thwarts. His strongest feeling must have been thankfulness to find the deck of the *Zwicker* under his feet once more.

"At eight o'clock we made sail and shaped our course for Seal Island, which we reached at four A.M."

By six o'clock that same evening, the *Zwicker* had beat into the majestic entrance of the lovely LaHave River and anchored with twenty fathom of chain. That closed the episode as far as

Captain Publicover was concerned. Of course, he logged the incident in the "Remarks" for December 20, as the law requires, without waste of words or undue display of emotion. The entry reads, in part:

"This day comes in blowing a gale of wind and a heavy sea running, put out a boat and rescued the crew of a distressed vessel, it being very dangerous work."

But Captain Publicover was not allowed to be the grave of his own deserving. Captain Sprague was passed up the river with his men to the care of the American consular agent at Bridgewater. No seal was on his lips, and he put the whole affair in a different light, when he made his official report to Mr. S. A. Chesley.

"Although in the face of the storm and terrible seas then prevailing the attempt seemed perfect folly," Publicover and Richard did, in fact, what they set out to do.

"The dangers of the transference," continues Captain Sprague, "were almost indescribable, and the heroism of the two men who accomplished it beyond praise."

Five months later, at Mr. Chesley's instance, Captain Publicover made a sworn statement before him of the facts as related and attested a copy of the entries in the log. Mr. Chesley, in turn, made representations to the American consul at Lunenburg. And in the end, the Lunenburg captain got his watch from President Wilson, and Fred Richard a gold medal, with an inscription on one side and a woman's head on the other, "in recognition of his heroic services."

A tropical scene. Sketch by Donald Mackay, from Tales of the Sea.

THE SHELL

Though he always attended the Presbyterian church when home at Maitland between voyages, and though he read his Bible regularly when at sea, Captain Jim Ellis did not believe in foreign missions. A waste of time and money, he declared. But circumstances over which he had absolutely no control led him to change his mind.

The Ellises were a large family living at Shubenacadie, the headquarters of Le Loutre in the olden days, whence supplies were brought down that turbulent river to the shipyards scattered along the shore of Cobequid Basin from Five Mile River to Maitland, Selma, Noel, and the rest. Jim Ellis was a poor boy, but William Lawrence, the great shipbuilder, singled him out for his ability and character to command his vessels. It was Jim Ellis who sailed the great ship, the *W. D. Lawrence*, on her famous fortune-making voyage round the world. Like the Industrious Apprentice, he married his master's daughter and made many prosperous voyages in the rolling *Pegasus,* a well-known Lawrence ship. Then he was promoted to command a big iron English ship, the *Ancona*, and his luck changed.

On May 5, 1892, he found himself off Bougainville Island, the largest of the Solomons. His *Sailing Directions* were clear about giving these islands a wide berth. The inhabitants were savage, treacherous headhunters and cannibals. Theirs was a black record. In 1854, they had murdered a whole boat's crew of HMS *Sandfly,* survey ship. When the yacht *Wanderer* was quietly at anchor in one of their harbours, all on board mysteriously disappeared. And there were gruesome tales of murdered missionaries.

In the night, the wind had failed and the heavy tropical rain poured down. The *Ancona* lay like a log on the sea, rolling on the heavy swell, all her gear clamouring and the water dripping from her sails. With the cloudy tropical dawn, a swarm of canoes put off from the shore and made for the motionless *Ancona*. Swiftly paddled, the tall, crescent-shaped prows inlaid with shell and mother-of-pearl came dipping over the foamless waves and were soon alongside. Then little, black, bushy-headed, naked men with runaway chins poured over the *Ancona*'s bulwarks and covered her decks. Every man carried a spear, or club, or bow, and quiverful of poisoned arrows. Ellis and his crew were helpless in their hands. There were no firearms of any kind on board, not a shotgun, not a revolver. Even if every one of the crew had been well armed, resistance would have been hopeless.

Captain Fred Ladd, on his honeymoon voyage, had to arm his crew to repel Malay pirates, but there was no fight.

Fear is generally a stranger to the heart of the Nova Scotian sea captain, but now, though there was no sign of it on his face, fear laid its grip on Captain Jim Ellis. What was the object of these unwelcome visitors? What did they want? They were running about everywhere, examining everything on deck, peering into the galley, the men's quarters forward, climbing about the rigging. They seemed filled with endless curiosity about the strange big canoe. They were picking up odds and ends.

They could not be fought with. Could they be bribed?

He consulted with his mate.

"Try 'em with food, Mr. Brierly," he said. "Don't stint 'em!"

So the cook and steward began handing out supplies from the lazarette, ship's bread and canned goods, opening the tins of meat and jam and passing them as fast as they could to the reaching black hands. The savages ate greedily, smearing their faces with the contents of the tins, and talking all the time in their curious, low-pitched, monotonous voices. There was something sinister in this flow of strange speech no one could understand. Captain Ellis had spoken to them first in English, without response. His few words of Samoan were just as unintelligible. Apparently there was nothing to do but try to fill their savage maws with food.

One man, obviously the chief, attached himself to Ellis and followed him about like his shadow. The burly Nova Scotian could have choked the life out of him in two minutes; the desperate thought even crossed his mind of seizing him and holding him for ransom, but a moment's reflection showed the futility of his wild scheme. A hostile motion towards the head man would have meant a massacre. Ellis wondered when the clubs and lances would come into play and the poisoned arrows be fitted to the bow-strings. Nothing seemed to satisfy the unwelcome visitors. They showed no sign of taking their leave.

Most of them seemed afraid to enter the various doors of the deck-house. They would peer into the dimness but they would venture no farther into what might be the white man's trap. The chief showed greater curiosity and less fear. He went up on the poop and into the pilot-house. Ellis had no choice but to accompany him. The ill-sorted pair went down the companionway to the mess room, which the chief explored thoroughly, then into the saloon which was a new wonder. By signs he made the captain understand that he must always precede him. The saloon with its couch, especially the resiliency of the springs, seemed to interest him. Seeing a door on the further side of the saloon, he motioned the white man to open it, and the two were in the third room of the series, the captain's own private stateroom. There the head man saw something that threw him into a state of the wildest excitement; he pointed, he jabbered, he gesticulated. What roused him was the ship's Bible lying open on the captain's desk where he had been reading his regular morning chapter.

Who can follow the processes of the savage mind? What thoughts passed through the brain of this savage chief? Other white men in big canoes traded. This buckra captain gave with both hands from his wonderful stores of riches and asked nothing in return. Why? Because he was a good man and followed the precepts of the good book. Now everything was plain. The book was the answer to the riddle.

The chief's excitement increased. Always with the sibilant hum of his strange speech, he explained by means of vivid pantomime, that a man, a white man, an old man with a long beard had come to his island in a big canoe like this and taught him and his people from this book. It was a good book—a good book. He made that plain. And then he hurried on deck, followed by the bewildered Ellis. He said something to the tribesmen which produced instant silence and he pointed to Captain Ellis. Making him understand by signs that he would soon return, he jumped into his canoe which was swiftly paddled to the shore. Ellis was mystified but the cloud of his anxiety lifted. The intent of the savages was not murder and plunder.

From the quarterdeck the captain of the *Ancona* eagerly watched the course of the canoe to shore. Above it towered the volcanic cones of mountains seven thousand feet high with cloud about their summits. In a short time it was returning as swiftly as the crew could paddle. It was hardly alongside before the chief was on the deck, kneeling at Ellis's feet and pouring out a flood of strange humming hissing speech. In his hand he held some small object wrapped in a dirty piece of old sail-cloth which he evidently regarded as very precious. Slowly he unwound the outer wrapper, showing a roll of grass fibre. Unwinding this with much ceremony, he showed a roll of leaves, and then Ellis found himself looking at the precious object—a small yellow seashell lying in the black palm.

He wanted to laugh—desperately. The sense of relief was almost too much. But the headman was intensely earnest, and the smeary faces of the silent, crowding, mop-headed savages were set and grave. Danger was not passed. Evidently what the chief was doing was most important. Ellis felt that even now a false move would be fatal; he must overcome the desperate impulse to giggle, and he fixed his eyes and his attention steadily on the shell.

It was cone-shaped, about five inches long, slender, graceful, the end suggesting an opening rosebud. The ground colour was pale ivory overlaid with a mosaic of thousands of tiny triangular figures of different sizes. These triangles were outlined in chrome yellow or deep chestnut brown. Ellis counted three broad spiral bands of orange encircling the body whorl beneath this fretted pattern. The longer he looked at it, the better he liked it. It was certainly a pretty shell. On the chief's black palm it had a lustre like porcelain suffused with faint rose. It almost mesmerized Captain Ellis.

At last the incomprehensible harangue came to an end. The chief made the captain know that he was to have the treasure, and Ellis received it with bows and smiles and many hand-shakings. In return, the Nova Scotian made him a special present of tobacco and saw him over the side, and he and all his tribe took a friendly leave. Patterson had not died in vain, nor had Atkin writhed for hours in the agonies of tetanus without resulting good. The clouds parted, the wind came up and filled the *Ancona*'s sails. She gathered way and soon the green shores of the island faded. By noon, the conical mountains were below the sea-rim.

Four weeks later, Captain Ellis sat in the verandah of the hotel at Hong Kong talking to a stranger. He was an American, a great traveller, who had been all over the world in the interests of a famous museum in the United States. His department was conchology; he was collecting shells of all kinds. He was a good talker; he knew everything about shells; he had been in the game all his life; his conversation had all the fascination of a specialist discoursing on his specialty. At last the captain said, "I've a specimen myself. Would you like to see it?"

The American was eager. The captain went to his room and brought down the chief's gift to the verandah. The American took it carelessly, looked at it nonchalantly, carried it over to the light, and examined the little yellow shell through the lenses of a pocket microscope, turning it over and over.

"Yes," he said, as he returned to his chair by the captain's side, "it's not a bad specimen of the—" and he pronounced some words in a foreign language a simple seaman could not be expected to understand. "I'll give you ten dollars for it."

Natural caution and ingrained Nova Scotian thrift made the captain hesitate. He said nothing. The stranger went on,

"I'll make it twenty-five."

Ellis seemed to catch a shade of eagerness in his tone, and he shook his head. "No," he said slowly, "I don't think I want to sell it."

188

"I'll give you fifty," said the stranger, reading Ellis's refusal as hesitation, and now there was no doubt of his eagerness. "I'll give you anything you like."

There was something in the stranger's manner Ellis did not like. "He put my back up," he said, in telling the tale.

"'No,' I said, 'I'm going to keep it for my little girl.'"

Captain Ellis has long since done with the sea and lies in Maitland churchyard. His little girl has a girl of her own who is ready for college, and she still treasures the chief's gift, the yellow shell, which her father brought home from the Solomons.

In the eighteenth century, *Conus Gloria Maris* was cherished by Dutch collectors. It is one of the rarest and loveliest things in the world. Kwass bought one at auction, paying a fabulous price. He crushed it under his heel, saying:

"Now I possess the only specimen in the world."

He was wrong. There are three specimens known to the conchologists. One is in the Museum of Natural History. Its acquisition was so important that the museum issued a special descriptive bulletin. But there is a fourth uncatalogued example of "The Glory of the Sea," the keepsake of a Maitland captain's daughter.

A privateer gives chase, 1851. Painting by an unknown artist.

THE BALLAD OF THE *ROVER*

Come, all you jolly sailor lads, that love the cannon's roar,
Your good ship on the briny wave, your lass and glass ashore,
How Nova Scotia's sons can fight you presently shall hear,
And of gallant Captain Godfrey in the Rover privateer.

She was a brig of Liverpool, of just a hundred tons;
She had a crew of fifty-five and mounted fourteen guns;
When south against King George's foes she first began to steer,
A smarter craft ne'er floated than the Rover privateer.

Five months our luck held good all up and down the Spanish Main;
And many a prize we overhauled and sent to port again;
Until the Spaniards laid their plans with us to interfere,
And stop the merry cruising of the Rover privateer.

The year was eighteen hundred, September tenth the day,
As off Cape Blanco in a calm all motionless we lay,
When the schooner Santa Ritta and three gunboats did appear,
A-sweeping down to finish off the Rover privateer.

With muskets and with pistols we engaged them as they came,
Till they closed in port and starboard, to play the boarding game;
Then we manned the sweeps and spun her round without a
    thought of fear,
And raked the Santa Ritta from the Rover privateer.

At once we spun her back again; the gunboats were too close;·
But our gunners they were ready, and they gave the Dons their dose.
They kept their distance after that and soon away did sheer,
And left the Santa Ritta to the Rover privateer.

We fought her for three glasses, and then we went aboard,
Our gallant captain heading us with pistol and with sword;
It did not take very long her bloody deck to clear,
And down came the Spanish colours to the Rover privateer.

We brought our prizes safe to port—we never lost a man;
There never was a luckier cruise since cruising first began; .
We fought and beat four Spaniards—now did you ever hear
The like of Captain Godfrey and the Rover privateer?

NOTES ON SOURCES

The following notes are compiled from the sources indicated by MacMechan in the contents pages of *Sagas of the Sea, Old Province Tales,* and *There Go the Ships.* For more information on his primary and secondary sources, consult the MacMechan papers in the Dalhousie University Archives.

The Captain's Boat
Information given to the San Francisco *Chronicle* by Captain MacArthur, and the interview of Mrs. MacArthur; Mr. E. S. Anthony of Coxsackie, N.Y. supplied many important details and read the story in manuscript.

At the Harbour Mouth
The Royal Gazette and The Nova Scotia Advertiser, Vol. IX, December 5, 1797. Hill, Rev. G. W. *Memoir of Sir Brenton Halliburton, Late Chief Justice of the Province of Nova Scotia* (Halifax: James Bowes & Sons, 1864), pp. 14–21.

The First Mate
Stenographic report from Captain Nehemiah C. Larkin's dictation, confirming notes of a previous interview given to the author.

Jordan the Pirate
Based on the account of the trial in the contemporary Halifax newspapers.

The Wave

Personal narrative and letters of Mrs. Hedley MacDougall; *La Razon* (Monte Video), May 18, 1901; *The Monte Video Times,* May 21, 1901; Report of Captain P. W. Sprague.

Via London

DesBrisay, Mather Byles. *History of the County of Lunenburg* (Toronto: William Briggs, 1895), pp. 242–245; Archives of Canada, Statement signed in London by survivors; Extracts from Gaetz's *Journal* kindly furnished by Mr. P. H. Ross of Lunenburg.

The *Saladin* Pirates

Trial of Jones, Hazelton, Anderson and Trevaskiss, alias Johnston, for piracy and murder, on board barque Saladin with the written confessions of the prisoners, produced in evidence on the said trial. To which is added, particulars of their execution on the 30th July. Also, the trial of Carr and Galloway, for the murder of Captain Fielding and his son, on board the Saladin, compiled from the Halifax papers (Halifax: James Bowes, 1844). Unique copy in Legislative Library, Halifax.

The Saga of "Rudder" Churchill

"An Example to Shipmasters," *The Times,* February 12, 1869; *The Times,* March 22, 1867; *The Glasgow Daily Herald,* February 6, March 21, 1867.

The *Sarah* Stands By

The Times, December 22, 25, 1849; January 4, 1850; *The New York Herald,* January 18, 25, 1850; *The Yarmouth Herald,* April 27, May 4, 1897.

The Captain's Wife

Sworn testimony of Captain Curry MacDougall, Mrs. MacDougall, H. R. Bowyer, and Thomas Desmond, used in the trial of the mutineers at Hong Kong; *The Hong Kong Telegraph,* April 9, 11, 18, 1895; Correspondence of Mrs. MacDougall.

The Lunenburg Way

Personal narrative of Captain James L. Publicover; Letter of Frederick Richard; Official documents.

The Shell

Information supplied by Mrs. F. E. O'Brien, the daughter of Captain James Ellis.

197

NOTES ON IMAGES

I

Archibald MacMechan, BA, Ph.D. Courtesy of the Archibald
MacMechan fonds, Dalhousie University Archives & Special
Collections, Halifax, NS. (Ref. PC1 17.53)

VIII

Archibald MacMechan (left) and Boyd Dunham with a model
of the *W. D. Lawrence*. Courtesy of the Archibald MacMechan
fonds, Dalhousie University Archives & Special Collections,
Halifax, NS. (Ref. PC2 8.14)

XIV

"The Captain's Boat." Sketch by Donald Mackay. Reprinted
from Archibald MacMechan, *Tales of the Sea*. Toronto:
McClelland & Stewart Limited, 1947, p. 209

Page 18

Painting of *La Tribune* and *Unicorn* in battle, 1796. Courtesy
of the Archibald MacMechan fonds, Dalhousie University
Archives & Special Collections, Halifax, NS. (Ref. PC2 8.10)

Page 30

Yarmouth waterfront. Courtesy of the Archibald MacMechan
fonds, Dalhousie University Archives & Special Collections,
Halifax, NS. (Ref. PC2 8.26)

Page 48

The *Arlington*. Courtesy of the Archibald MacMechan fonds, Dalhousie University Archives & Special Collections, Halifax, NS. (Ref. PC2 7.89)

Page 56

Captain John Stairs, 1842. Courtesy of the Archibald MacMechan fonds, Dalhousie University Archives & Special Collections, Halifax, NS. (Ref. PC2 7.81)

Page 68

Hedley and May MacDougall (née Cumming) at Yokohama, just after their marriage. Courtesy of the Archibald MacMechan fonds, Dalhousie University Archives & Special Collections, Halifax, NS. (Ref. MS 2 82 44.43)

Page 76

Dispatch box saved from schooner *Industry*, 1868. Courtesy of the Archibald MacMechan fonds, Dalhousie University Archives & Special Collections, Halifax, NS. (Ref. PC2 7.100)

Page 88

Stern decoration from the *Saladin*. Courtesy of the Archibald MacMechan fonds, Dalhousie University Archives & Special Collections, Halifax, NS. (Ref. PC2 8.2)

Page 106

The *Research* in a storm. Courtesy of the Archibald MacMechan fonds, Dalhousie University Archives & Special Collections, Halifax, NS. (Ref. PC2 7.108)

Page 126
The *Shannon* and the *Chesapeake*, triumphal entry into Halifax Harbour. Courtesy of the Archibald MacMechan fonds, Dalhousie University Archives & Special Collections, Halifax, NS. (Ref. PC2 7.94)

Page 140
"The *Sarah* Stands By." Sketch by Donald Mackay. Reprinted from Archibald MacMechan, *Tales of the Sea*. Toronto: McClelland & Stewart Limited, 1947, p. 127

Page 164
The *Launberga*, pen drawing from a picture postcard, C. R. Wilcox '27. Courtesy of the Archibald MacMechan fonds, Dalhousie University Archives & Special Collections, Halifax, NS. (Ref. PC2 7.102)

Page 174
W. N. Zwicker, schooner and rescue ship, 1902. Courtesy of the Archibald MacMechan fonds, Dalhousie University Archives & Special Collections, Halifax, NS. (Ref. PC2 8.12)

Page 182
"Jury-Rig." Sketch by Donald Mackay. Reprinted from Archibald MacMechan, *Tales of the Sea*. Toronto: McClelland & Stewart Limited, 1947, p. 69

Page 190
Painting of a privateer, 1851. Courtesy of the Archibald MacMechan fonds, Dalhousie University Archives & Special Collections, Halifax, NS. (Ref. PC2 9.2)